PRAISE FOR
THE STRATEGIC MONEY METHOD

"This book delivers practical tools wrapped in relatable stories that make complex financial ideas simple and usable. The three-step process is clear and surprisingly transformative. If you've ever felt stuck despite knowing the 'rules,' this is the guide that will finally help you move forward with confidence."

—RUSSELL N. JAMES III, JD, PhD, CFP®, professor, CH Foundation Chair of Personal Financial Planning, Charitable Giving Program Director, Texas Tech University

"*The Strategic Money Method* is a compass for rethinking how you spend, save, and plan—a clear, practical guide that empowers consumers to align money decisions with what truly matters."

—DR. CHARLES CHAFFIN, cofounder, Money and Risk Inventory; cofounder, Psychology of Financial Planning; professor, Iowa State University

"This book is highly informative, practical, and understandable for all types of readers interested in making better financial decisions. Patrick provides a wonderful perspective of the different psychological aspects experienced within the financial planning process. I especially enjoyed the discussion and presentation about investor personality."

—VICTOR RICCIARDI, coauthor, *Advanced Introduction to Behavioral Finance*

"Dr. Payne writes about personal finance with humor and humility. The strategies he offers are easy to read, easy to understand, and, most importantly, easy to implement. I highly recommend this book to anyone wanting to get a handle on their finances, as well as those in the personal finance industry who wish to reach their clientele in meaningful and effective ways. Dr. Payne takes what might otherwise be considered complex personal finance concepts and turns them into enjoyable and relatable stories that convey useful strategies for getting a handle on money matters. I plan to purchase enough copies of this book to give as gifts to my adult children, nieces, and nephews, who will no doubt gain from Dr. Payne's straightforward strategies embedded in relatable analogies and funny personal stories. I've worked my entire adult career in higher education and have come across only a handful of academicians who are able to convey complex concepts with an abundance of clarity and a healthy dose of humility. Dr. Payne has accomplished that!"

—**DR. DANIEL MCDONALD,** distinguished outreach professor, Take Charge America Endowed Chair, University of Arizona

"*The Strategic Money Method* offers a fresh perspective on personal finance, going beyond basic tips to explore the deeper logic behind financial decisions. Drawing from years of teaching, research, and real-life experiences, Dr. Patrick Payne provides a practical and accessible framework for making money choices that makes money decisions less overwhelming. Whether you are just starting your financial journey or looking to change your financial path, this book can help you. Dr. Payne's empowering perspective and clear writing make the book a valuable guide for anyone seeking to make smarter and more intentional financial decisions."

—**JOHN GRABLE,** PhD, CFP®, Athletic Association Endowed FACS Professor, Department of Financial Planning, University of Georgia

"While it seems easier in personal finance to start with the rules, or rules of thumb, unless we start with the vision of where we want our finances to take us, we won't likely get where we want to be. Patrick Payne helps us see the importance of first having our own unique strategy or vision, then gives us tools through his three key questions to keep us moving toward fulfilling that strategy. By following his guidance, this book will positively impact your personal finances."

—**BARRY S. MULHOLLAND**, PhD, CFP®, ChFC®, clinical associate professor, W. P. Carey School of Business, Arizona State University

"Patrick Payne's *The Strategic Money Method* has done it! Finally, a commonsense, thoughtful approach to the art and science of financial planning. As Dr. Payne writes, 'You cannot create an effective plan until you first establish a solid strategy.' This book ensures the reader has all the tools to establish both the plan and the strategy. A must-read for all those looking to build and maintain wealth."

—**KIM DANIELS WALSH**, JD, associate professor of practice, Personal and Family Financial Planning, University of Arizona; of counsel, Schenck, Price, Smith & King

"A clear-headed approach to financial decision-making. By putting vision before goals and strategy before tactics, you will learn to plan your financial life in a way that can get you where you want to go and easily adapt to life's inevitable changes along the way."

—**SARAH NEWCOMB**, PhD, author of *Loaded: Money, Psychology, and How to Get Ahead Without Leaving Your Values Behind*

"This is a well-written, easy-to-read book that demystifies the financial decision-making process. It provides practical, understandable advice that can be applied to any reader's individual goals and values. Rather than following a one-size-fits-all rule, readers identify their personal strategy and then create a plan to implement that strategy."

—**CHARLENE M. KALENKOSKI**, PhD, CFP®, dean, School of Business and Communication, Mount St. Joseph University

"For over a decade, I have been looking for a relevant resource to help my students go beyond financial definitions and rules of thumb for money decisions. *The Strategic Money Method* is just that resource, and it is certain to become a class favorite. In a very practical and relatable way, Payne describes effective approaches to financial decision-making."

—**JACOB A. TENNEY**, PhD, CFP®, associate professor, University of Charleston

"*The Strategic Money Method* presents three realistic questions, each with in-depth explanations, to guide your thought process in financial decision-making. It clearly shows how these questions interconnect and empowers you to apply them with confidence."

—**THOMAS KORANKYE**, PhD, CFP®, EA, assistant professor, Personal and Family Financial Planning, University of Arizona

"*The Strategic Money Method* is a refreshing take on personal finance. Instead of quick tips or rigid rules, it equips readers with a clear, practical framework for making smarter financial choices. This book helps you align money decisions with your values and long-term goals."

—**CHRIS BROWNING**, PhD, CFP®, associate professor, Texas Tech University; national director, Financial Planning Academy

"Most money books tell you what to do. This one teaches you how to think. With over a decade of experience teaching thousands of college students, Dr. Patrick Payne understands that sound financial decisions come from knowing ourselves—not just following financial rules. By combining psychological insights and practical strategies, he explores the emotional roadblocks that derail our best financial intentions and shares methods for overcoming them. Through a simple framework of self-reflective questions and actionable sections on empowered spending, intentional borrowing, and efficient investing, this book offers a personalized and holistic approach to money management that actually works!"

—**VICTORIA LIGON**, PhD, associate professor of practice, Personal and Family Financial Planning, University of Arizona

The Strategic Money Method moves beyond numbers and generic rules that dominate financial advice. Patrick Payne helps readers rethink money at a deeper level, offering a framework that tailors decisions to personal values and long-term goals—equipping them with the confidence and practical tools to finally master their money."

—**JACOB WILLIAMS**, PhD, CFP®, director, Planning and Research, Helmstar Wealth Management

"With memorable metaphors and actionable step-by-step playbooks for spending, borrowing, and investing, *The Strategic Money Method* replaces guesswork with confidence in everyday financial decisions."

—**BLAIN PEARSON**, PhD, CFP®, assistant professor of finance and economics, Coastal Carolina University

THE
STRATEGIC
MONEY METHOD

DISCOVER THE HIDDEN LOGIC BEHIND
BETTER FINANCIAL DECISIONS

PATRICK PAYNE, PhD, CFP®

Kiplinger BOOKS

This publication is designed to provide accurate and authoritative information in regard to the subject matter covered. It is sold with the understanding that the publisher and author are not engaged in rendering legal, accounting, or other professional services. Nothing herein shall create an attorney-client relationship, and nothing herein shall constitute legal advice or a solicitation to offer legal advice. If legal advice or other expert assistance is required, the services of a competent professional should be sought.

Kiplinger Books
New York, New York
www.kiplinger.com

This work is being published under the Kiplinger Books imprint by an exclusive arrangement with Future US LLC. Kiplinger and the Kiplinger logo are registered trademarks of Future US LLC. The Kiplinger Books logo is a wholly owned trademark of Future US LLC.

Distributed by River Grove Books

Design and composition by Greenleaf Book Group
Cover design by Greenleaf Book Group

Publisher's Cataloging-in-Publication data is available.

Print ISBN: 978-1-969190-04-9

eBook ISBN: 978-1-969190-05-6

First Edition

CONTENTS

INTRODUCTION

I love efficiency—in all things, but especially in my cars. I don't just want a car that runs; I want a car that does everything it's supposed to do with as little waste as possible. No useless extra buttons. No tiny scraps of plastic that block my view but perform no function. Every vehicle I've ever purchased had to check a very specific set of boxes: It needed to be compact enough to maneuver easily and park anywhere, have flexible and well-designed interior space, offer ample storage, and, of course, get excellent gas mileage. That's why I love the idea of hybrid cars. They represent thoughtful design and the smart use of resources; leveraging the advantages of gas and the advantages of electric, as well as a commitment to doing more with less.

In many ways, that's how I think about money, too.

Personal finance is like a hybrid car: part psychology, part finance. It doesn't fully belong in either category, but it draws on elements from both.

You can't find financial success with just economic models and financial math. Nor can you rely only on behavioral theories and emotional insights. You need to understand how dollars and decisions work together—how motivation, emotion, and relationships intertwine with numbers, budgets, and strategy to power the financial engine of a real person's life.

The blended nature of personal finance is one of the things I love most about this field, but that characteristic also makes it a bit of an ugly duckling in the academic world.

As a professor of financial planning, I train students to become Certified Financial Planners® every day. Part of this requires me to keep an eye on the schools that offer this still rather new field of study. As a subject that draws from the worlds of both business and psychology, personal finance straddles both domains while fully fitting into neither one. I have seen personal finance programs placed all over college campuses, including in some truly surprising departments, like agriculture, medicine, and even, in one odd instance, fine arts! For the most part, however, these programs wind up being hosted in one of two places: the business school or the school of human sciences.

Business schools and finance programs often don't feel like personal finance belongs with them because it seems too touchy-feely. Corporate finance people often see themselves as masters of complex mathematics and unsolvable equations. The better their financial models, the more profitable they can be. Their field is about making money for the sake of making money. The money is the point. Financial planners deal with people, and that's just not finance's purview. They don't deal with emotion—they prefer cash. "Go play with the psychology people and leave us to our calculations," they say.

The psychologists and human behaviorists, too, sometimes turn their nose up at financial planners. Their perspective is often that we financial-planning folks deal in money, while they view themselves as the keepers of the higher, nobler arts of human happiness. They are the authorities on healthy marriages, happy families, positive mental health, and overall human well-being. They don't want to dirty their hands with something as crass as money.

Think about it. Where do you find books on personal finance in the bookstore or library? Where did you find the book you hold in your hands at this very moment? No doubt some of you found it in business and finance. Others doubtless discovered it while perusing the shelves of the self-help section.

The truth is that personal finance is at its best when it embraces its multifaceted nature. Fortunately, those general attitudes I described before are not universal, and there are many people from all walks of life and areas of specialization that recognize and celebrate the hybrid nature of personal finance. That's been the case at all the universities and departments where I have taught: My colleagues, regardless of their field of expertise, have embraced this subject, and everyone's students benefited.

When I taught in business schools, I leveraged the expertise of the accountants to help my students better study taxes, and I called upon the marketing faculty to lend their mastery of the psychology of buying. When I taught in human science departments, my family counseling colleagues lent my students their skill in helping couples navigate conflicting financial priorities; the child development faculty taught my students how to teach clients how to help their own children and grandchildren learn important life lessons of all kinds. In turn, I taught the family counseling students how money affects relationships, and ways to structure finances that can help ease tensions within families. Our fields of study are better together.

Yes, I truly love the multidisciplinary nature of personal finance.

It keeps me on my toes. It lets me learn so much about such a broad portion of the human experience. Money touches every part of our lives, whether we think it should or not.

Unfortunately, this hybrid nature is also the aspect of personal finance that makes it so tremendously challenging for most people to understand and manage. It's not enough to understand taxes. You also have to understand mutual fund expense ratios, and insurance deductibles, and the importance of having a will. You have to manage your own emotional and physical needs. How do you fight down the urge to buy the latest tech gadget when you know you don't need it but want it anyway? You will also benefit from understanding how to work towards shared, individual, and family financial goals with your partner.

Little wonder that so many of us struggle immensely with our money.

It seems like it should be so simple. Just spend less than you earn. Invest what you don't spend. Enjoy a glorious retirement. Live happily ever after. The end.

But it's not that simple, is it? If it were, you wouldn't have picked up this book. You wouldn't have read through this meandering introduction. You wouldn't be wondering if this guy is ever going to get to the point.

Okay, fair enough. I'll cut to the chase.

There are millions of books out there offering to help you with your money. The internet is teeming with experts to give you advice. Some of them are actually experts, some don't have a clue, and some are just predators hoping to make a quick buck.

Even the best experts struggle with a similar problem. That problem? They are experts in just one area of personal finance. One guru may be great at helping you get out of debt, but their relationship advice leaves something to be desired. Another might be great at psychology and relationships but can offer only superficial advice on investing. A third could be a great investor but can't fill out a simple tax form. And another is a tax genius but doesn't know much about getting out of debt.

I have the advantage of an education and real-life experience that's comprehensive and runs deep. I spent four years getting my PhD in personal financial planning at Texas Tech University (go Red Raiders!). It was a magical experience. As a lifelong nerd, I thrived in an environment where I could study at the highest levels all the topics of personal finance: behavioral biases, mental heuristics, investment strategies, tax efficiencies, legislative policies, micro- and macro-economics, statistics, relationship dynamics, retirement planning law, estate planning law, common and contract law, and on and on.

I won't claim to be a foremost expert in all of these areas. There are fabulous researchers and professionals who specialize deeply in their fields who can stump me. I respect these folks immensely.

My specialization is a little different. I specialize in teaching—in hybrid teaching, to be exact. I have spent the past twelve years teaching personal finance to students of all levels. I have spent every single one of those years focused intensely on one question above all others: How do I teach the most important lessons of financial planning in a way that empowers but doesn't overwhelm? The scientific evidence on the effectiveness of financial literacy education is mixed at best. The conclusion is that it has to be done *just so* in order to effectively give people the ability to improve their financial situation. Otherwise, it's just wasting everyone's time.

After having taught thousands of students, heard their feedback, and followed up with them over the years, I have focused in on the financial principles and educational processes that give students the ability to think critically about financial decisions. The results have been very rewarding to see in the classroom.

When I first started teaching, students provided very robotic answers. Exactly the kinds of answers you would expect from a traditional classroom experience. So over time, I have evolved my teaching methods and topics, honing my lectures and assignments every single semester and gauging the reactions of students. The results have been worth the effort. Students now come up with novel solutions to financial questions their "client" is facing. They crunch the numbers, think outside the box, and identify risks and advantages to strategies. In short, they now show far more critical thinking ability after my class than the students in my first class ever did.

This means I have blended together the key elements of different fields so I can provide a complete set of tools for understanding personal finance. These tools help students apply the principles of personal finance to their own unique lives. I want to give that training experience to all of you and not be limited just to those students who have the chance to sit in my classroom at university.

The philosophy of this book is simple: You don't need to know everything about money to be successful at financial planning. You just need to change the way you think. Instead of developing lists of dos and don'ts or memorizing rules and techniques, you need to think about money more strategically and consider a few key questions about every financial decision.

A financial strategy doesn't have to be complex. If you can understand a few key principles, adjust your methods, and focus on doing just a handful of things correctly throughout your life, you can achieve 90 percent of the benefits of full financial mastery without being overwhelmed by the sheer volume of knowledge available in financial planning. For example, you don't need to worry about picking winning stocks or watching your portfolio of investments. I'll show you why.

Let me be clear—this isn't about cutting corners. I'm not going to suggest that ignorance is good. It'll take work to rewire the way you think about money and financial decisions. Rather, it's about focusing on what matters most and freeing yourself from the unnecessary noise that often dominates personal finance education—stuff like the difference between money market funds and high-yield savings accounts, or how your 403(b) retirement plan differs from your neighbor's 401(k) plan. The details can be helpful for those who have the time and inclination to chase them, but for the vast majority of us, they represent a high-effort, low-reward endeavor. Instead, this book is about empowering you to take action with confidence, knowing that you don't need to have all the answers to create a secure financial future.

THE PROBLEM WITH TRADITIONAL FINANCIAL EDUCATION

Think about how personal finance is typically taught. In a classroom, you're handed a long list of facts, rules, and strategies to memorize; things like the different types of debt, the intricacies of investment accounts, or how to optimize Social Security benefits. While these details are certainly part of the process, and you need a baseline of facts and vocabulary to even get started studying any topic, the sheer volume means that these facts often end up being more overwhelming than helpful. If you're learning from a book rather than in a classroom, you may be told the "best" way to do something and then be left to your own devices to go and do it. The problem is that there truly isn't a "best" way to do anything. No rule applies 100 percent of the time. You will inevitably find yourself as the exception, and you may not even realize it. Personally, I've never read a personal finance book that teaches you how to think about money; usually, the focus seems to be telling you what to do with money.

So I wrote a book to do just that: teach you how to think about money. (It's the book you're holding right now, just in case that wasn't clear.)

Let's look at a quick example to give you an idea of what I'm talking about. Let's take debt management, for example. Instead of memorizing the differences between revolving and amortizing debt or learning every nuance of fixed- versus adjustable-rate mortgages (or learning to never use debt at all), what if you focused on one core principle? Debt buys you time. It allows you to get what you want or need *now*, but it comes at a cost. Understanding that cost and weighing it against the benefits, both financial and psychological, of using debt is far more empowering than memorizing technical definitions or blindly following the "rules."

THE DANGER OF OVERSIMPLIFICATION

While excessive detail can paralyze us, oversimplification can mislead us. Many financial educators rely on catchy slogans like "All debt is bad" or "Invest as early as possible." These sound straightforward and are generally not bad ideas. However, they are fundamentally flawed, because they don't account for the unique challenges and circumstances we each face.

Take the advice to avoid carrying a balance on your credit card. That's great in theory, but what about someone who has to choose between groceries and paying off their balance? Or the advice to invest early: It ignores the reality that many young people struggle just to cover their bills, let alone set aside money for retirement. These oversimplified rules create guilt and frustration when life inevitably forces us to break them.

This book takes a different approach. Instead of giving you a checklist of dos and don'ts, it will teach you a way to think about money. Principles and frameworks stick with you far longer than facts or slogans ever could. By *understanding* why certain financial decisions work, and by learning how to evaluate your own unique circumstances, you'll be equipped to handle life's financial twists and turns with confidence.

Financial literacy isn't about memorizing rules; it's about strategically pursuing your goals and building a method for analyzing decisions, developing plans, and then making those plans a reality. When you know how to approach financial decisions thoughtfully and systematically, you'll feel empowered to make the best choices for your life—even when they go against conventional wisdom.

WHAT IS THE STRATEGIC MONEY METHOD?

The Strategic Money Method is exactly what it sounds like: a clear and practical system for making financial decisions that support the life you actually want to live. This method begins with defining your vision and purpose in order to give you a sense of direction with your money, rather than the feeling that you're simply reacting to your financial circumstances. From there, you'll learn to apply three key questions to every financial choice, which will help you focus on what truly matters; you'll learn how to weigh costs and benefits and avoid distractions that pull you off course. With this foundation in place, we'll build out the rest of the strategy by creating a spending plan rooted in intentionality, learning how to use credit as a tool instead of a trap and how to invest with clarity and confidence. All together, these pieces form a flexible yet powerful method for managing your financial life with strategy instead of stress: the Strategic Money Method.

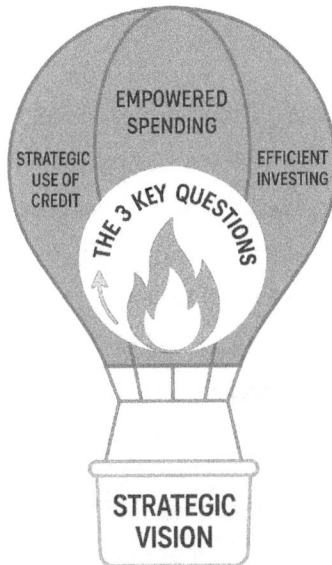

FIGURE 0.1. Financial Life as a Hot Air Balloon

One way to understand the Strategic Money Method is to picture your financial life as a hot air balloon. This image captures how all the pieces of this method work together to lift your financial life and give it a sense of progress and direction. At the base is the basket, which represents your strategic vision. It holds you and everything that matters most to you: Your goals, values, priorities, and purpose are all carried here. Without a basket, you're not a hot air balloon at all—you're just a tarp flapping in the wind, getting snagged on trees and tumbling wherever life blows you. You might still move, but it won't be intentional, satisfying, or safe.

But a grounded vision alone won't get you into the air. You need lift. That's where the three key questions come in. Like the fire and fuel of a hot air balloon, these questions drive the whole system. They help you think strategically, evaluate your trade-offs, and make decisions with clarity. They're not a step in the process, they're the constant heat that keeps your financial life rising.

Then there's the balloon itself, the visible part that actually takes flight. It's made up of the tools and tactics that carry you upward: empowered spending that reflects your values, strategic use of credit that protects and extends your resources, and efficient investing that grows your wealth for the long haul. Each of these components contributes to your lift. But they only work when they're connected to a solid foundation and fueled by intentional decision-making. In the same way a balloonist adjusts the flame to respond to changing winds, you'll use this method to make real-time decisions as life evolves.

Here's what you can expect to learn in these pages:

- The key elements of developing a focused, coherent, and successful financial strategy

- How to adjust your mindset to build lifetime financial security without feeling deprived

- A simple three-question approach to making better, more efficient financial choices with ease
- A simple method for making smart choices in spending, borrowing, and investing

Whether you're just starting out, are in mid-career, or are nearing retirement, this book will help you simplify your financial life and focus on what really matters. By the end, you'll have the tools, the confidence, and the clarity to build a lifetime of financial security and satisfaction.

Let's get started.

PART I

STRATEGIC THINKING

CHAPTER ONE

THE FOUNDATIONS OF FINANCIAL STRATEGY

V ictory was assured.

We were a few turns into a game of Settlers of Catan when I realized my friend—let's call him Brian—had no strategy. It was his first time playing, and I'd given him the basic rules: collect resources, build settlements and roads, try to get to ten points. That's it.

If you're not familiar, Settlers of Catan is a classic board game built around trading, building, and expanding a small civilization using the resources available on the game board. At the start of the game, the rules make your objective clear: Reach ten victory points before anyone else. That's the goal.

And Brian? He was having a blast collecting resources and smugly building a sprawling empire. Every time he got enough cards, he'd buy something—anything. Didn't matter if it fit a strategy or not. Brick and lumber? Build a road. Wheat and ore? Upgrade to a city. Got a sheep? Might as well trade it for something. He was like a kid in a candy store, gleefully collecting and spending without ever thinking about where he was trying to go.

The problem was his board was a mess. Roads that led nowhere. Settlements in low-yield spots. No path to the Longest Road bonus, no chance at claiming the Largest Army bonus, and no clear plan to reach ten points. He built a ton of stuff, but none of it worked together. His efforts were scattered—and in the end, so were his points.

I didn't say anything. I could have jumped in, given him tips, helped him think more strategically. But I didn't. Some lessons are best learned the hard way.

As the game ended and he looked at the board, he finally saw it.

"Wait," he said, "I built all this stuff and I barely scored any points?" Yep. That's how it works when you build without a strategy. It takes work and looks productive, but it doesn't get you where you want to go.

And honestly, it's not that different from the way a lot of us approach money. We spend, we save, we hustle, we accumulate—and if we're not careful, we end up with a lot of financial activity that doesn't actually move us closer to anything meaningful. That's why a clear financial vision—and the strategy that follows—is so important. Without it, we're just rolling dice and hoping for the best.

How about you? Are you approaching your finances with a clear strategy, or just reacting to each situation as it comes? Many people I meet who feel stuck financially aren't making decisions with a long-term purpose in mind. They're doing their best in the moment—buying what they want when there's money in the bank or room on the credit card—without considering how those choices shape their future. If that sounds familiar, don't worry. You're not alone, and you've picked up the right book.

A major problem that a lot of people have is that they try to make financial decisions without first sitting down to identify their strategy. You can't take control of your finances until you have a clear idea of what you would like your money to do for you. A financial strategy is the right tool for the job.

I talk about strategy before I talk about plans for a simple reason: A plan is essentially a detailed set of steps or actions designed to achieve a specific outcome. It's about laying out what you're going to do and when you're going to do it. Think of it as your road map—precise, clear, and focused on implementation.

On the other hand, a strategy involves making critical choices that determine the direction, and the ultimate success, of your plan. A strategy is about setting priorities, deciding where to allocate resources, and understanding the trade-offs involved. A strategy is focused on the reasons behind your actions; it guides your decisions and helps you navigate uncertainties. While a plan is about execution, a strategy positions you to succeed in the long run.

What does this look like for a board game like Settlers of Catan? What did I do that Brian didn't?

My strategy was to focus on controlling the most valuable resource tiles. Fast expansion is often a winning formula in this game, so I specifically prioritized securing access to brick and wood early on. This let me box Brian out so that he couldn't access the other resources he needed to score points. That was my big-picture strategic approach: dominate early resource control of brick and wood so I could expand faster than Brian, seize other resources, and control the board.

Now that I had a strategy, I could start planning. A plan is how you execute that strategy, turn by turn. It includes deciding where to place your initial settlements; when to prioritize building a road versus trading for resources; which opponents to make deals with (and which to avoid);

and even when to shift tactics if you are being blocked. The plan adjusts based on dice rolls, trades, and the evolution of the board, but it always serves your broader strategy of early expansion.

In essence, while a plan tells you how to get somewhere, a strategy helps you decide where you should be going and why. Your finances must first and foremost be thoroughly grounded in your personal sense of purpose. You cannot create an effective plan until you first establish a solid strategy. Without an underlying strategy, even a perfectly executed plan will lack direction and fail to deliver what you truly want.

COMPONENTS OF A FINANCIAL STRATEGY

Where does one start developing a financial strategy for their life? It doesn't start with knowing all the rules, although that can help.

Think of it like building a house. You don't start with the walls or even the foundation. You start with a blueprint. What are you trying to build? What should it look like when it's complete? That blueprint is your vision for your life: a picture of the life you want to live and the lifestyle you want your money to provide. Too many people haven't defined what they want their money to accomplish. The result is that they struggle to get somewhere, but without a direction, they inevitably wind up going nowhere. So step one of designing a financial strategy for your life is to define the vision or outcome you would like to achieve.

Once we have a clear vision of where to go, we need a strong foundation for decision-making. That foundation is the strategic money method I will be teaching you. It's the solid base upon which every financial decision is built—the process by which you decide which things to spend money on and which things to avoid. Without the foundation of a clear, effective, and strategic approach to your finances, even the best advice can crumble under the weight of life's complexities. But with these methods? You can weather challenges, adapt to changes, and build a life of stability and satisfaction.

RULES VERSUS STRATEGY

It's tempting to rely on simple financial rules, such as spend less than you earn, invest early, follow the 4 percent rule, or stick to 50/30/20 budgeting. These rules make managing money seem easy and well within reach.

While rules like these can be helpful starting points, they're not magic formulas. Real success comes from understanding the principles behind them, knowing when they apply and when they don't. That kind of thinking requires more than memorizing rules; it requires developing a money method for thinking strategically. To illustrate why that matters, let me tell you about the first time I tried to cook a brisket.

I followed the rule *perfectly*. I'd done the research, watched the YouTube gurus, read the BBQ blogs. I had the rub and the pellets; I had the smoker dialed in. And I had the rule: *One hour per pound at 225 degrees.*

Mine was a thirteen-pound beauty. I'm good at math, so I was able to apply the rule and calculate that thirteen hours was my cook time. I prepped like I was about to launch a space shuttle and got that brisket on the smoker just after midnight. Thirteen hours later, I pulled it off the heat. It looked great, with a nice, black, crunchy bark, just like in the videos. Unfortunately the beauty of my brisket was literally only skin deep. One bite revealed the horrifying truth: I hadn't smoked a brisket—I'd slow-cooked a leather belt.

I'd been betrayed! I'd followed the rule exactly. What went wrong?

I was complaining about this ordeal to my neighbor when they asked me the question that changed my entire perspective:

"Did you pull it at temp, or just by time?"

Oh.

Turns out brisket isn't done when the clock says it is—it's done when the thermometer says (somewhere around 195 to 200 degrees Fahrenheit). I'd been cooking by schedule, not science.

That's when I learned something bigger than BBQ:

RULES ARE TOOLS, NOT TRUTHS.

Whether it's about meat or money, blindly following a rule without understanding the why behind it can lead to chewy outcomes.

I don't have to be a true grill master to make a very respectable brisket. My brisket may not win against the pros in a state championship, but it satisfies my family every time. That's all I really ever wanted my brisket to accomplish. I don't need to become a master of fire and smoke to make a decent brisket. I just need to understand what matters and use the right tools—like a wireless thermometer—to get the job done well.

The same goes for money. You don't need to be a financial expert to succeed. You just need to embrace a few correct principles and learn how to think critically about money. Every financial decision, whether it's as big as buying a home or as small as choosing what to eat for lunch, can either bring you closer to or further away from the life you want to build. With a clear understanding of what truly matters to you, your decisions become more intentional, and your financial journey becomes a reflection of your values and aspirations.

The strategic money method that I will teach you in this book is the compass that points you in the right direction. It won't solve every problem for you, but it will give you the tools and perspective you need to navigate any situation. With the right approach to answering financial questions, you'll find that financial success isn't just possible—it's likely.

After teaching financial literacy to thousands of students, I've found that making smart financial decisions comes down to asking yourself three key questions. These three questions form the foundation of the money method that will drive your financial strategy; they will empower you to take greater control of all of your financial decisions, big and small.

THE THREE KEY QUESTIONS

Financial success doesn't come from earning more money or cutting expenses. It requires adopting the right mentality—one that empowers you to make sound decisions, grow your resources, and achieve your goals. This chapter introduces the three fundamental questions you should continually ask and answer in order to make sound financial decisions; decisions that serve your strategy for realizing your vision for your life. By incorporating these questions into the way you approach money decisions, you'll find yourself gradually becoming more financially empowered and making decisions that lead to success, however you define it.

These three questions are your foundation. Each provides a crucial piece of the puzzle, and together they form a complete method for approaching financial decisions with clarity and purpose. Here's a brief overview of each key question, which we will explore in greater depth in subsequent chapters.

KEY QUESTION 1: WHAT IS THE PURPOSE OF THIS PURCHASE?

The first key question is to ask yourself what you hope this particular purchase will accomplish for you. Every dollar you spend should serve a purpose, whether it's buying a home, a car, new clothes, or an investment.

The key question to ask yourself is: *What am I trying to accomplish with this purchase?*

Spending money shouldn't be accidental or impulsive. It should be intentional, aligning with your goals and values. This requires introspection and honesty. You need to understand yourself—your needs, desires, and priorities—to ensure your spending choices genuinely improve your life. When you focus on function, you stop wasting money on things that don't matter and start using your resources to create meaningful benefits.

KEY QUESTION 2: IS IT WORTH THE COST?

The second key question is to weigh costs and benefits by asking the question: *Is this worth what it costs?* It's not enough to ask yourself, *Can I afford this?* Instead, ask, *Should I pay this much for this thing?* It's not about whether you can buy something, but whether or not the value it provides is worth the price.

Evaluating costs and benefits involves both tangible and intangible factors. Calculating the tangible costs of a loan, investment, or purchase is straightforward—online calculators make it easy. The harder part is assessing the intangible costs and benefits: How much joy, convenience, or peace of mind will this bring? How will it align with your long-term goals? This key isn't about telling you what to want; it's about teaching you how to evaluate your decisions holistically to maximize benefits while minimizing costs.

KEY QUESTION 3: IS THERE A SMART SWAP?

Once you understand what you want to achieve with your money and how to weigh costs and benefits, you need to explore other options. Ask yourself, *Can I meet this need in a less expensive way?* There are always multiple ways to achieve a particular goal or fill a specific need. Identifying which ones provide the same or similar benefits at lower costs can save you tremendous amounts of money without negatively affecting your lifestyle.

For example, if your goal is to travel, you might find that a local vacation offers comparable enjoyment to an international trip but at a fraction of the cost. If you're looking to buy a car, comparing models or considering a used vehicle can help you achieve that goal for less cost. By expanding your options and thinking creatively, you'll often find that there's a better, more cost-effective way to reach your goals.

HOW THE QUESTIONS INTERACT

While each of the three key questions is essential on its own, they also overlap and interact in meaningful ways. For example, evaluating alternatives can only happen effectively when you have correctly identified the need you are trying to meet. Without understanding the function of a purchase, it's impossible to consider other ways to fulfill the same need. Similarly, weighing the costs and benefits is a crucial step for each alternative you evaluate. Every option has its own trade-offs, and careful comparison is necessary to determine which one aligns best with your goals and values. If you don't know the need you are trying to meet, you cannot evaluate the benefits of your choice.

This interplay means that these questions are not separate steps to be taken in isolation, but rather parts of a cohesive and ongoing process. Focusing on function grounds your decisions, weighing costs and benefits ensures thoughtful evaluation, and exploring alternatives broadens your options. Regularly asking yourself all three questions together creates a dynamic method that empowers you to make intentional financial decisions.

By mastering this process of questioning your financial decisions, you'll develop a financial mindset that sets you up for long-term success. Each of these principles is a skill you can refine with practice; together, they will help you navigate life's financial decisions with greater confidence, clarity and, most importantly, success. In the chapters ahead, we'll break down each question, show examples of how each one plays out in real life, and help you see the full process in action.

As you work to get used to thinking in this way, be patient with yourself. It takes time and consistent effort to form new mental habits—your brain is literally rewiring itself. But you *can* get there. I've seen it happen countless times. I've watched students who were terrible at math, who couldn't bring themselves to care about the stock market, and who would've died of boredom reading an insurance policy go on to master these concepts and make sharp, confident financial decisions.

They came from all walks of life: dancers and poets, engineers and scientists, athletes and mathletes. Some were outgoing, others quiet and introspective. Personality, background, or interests didn't matter. What they had in common wasn't a love for finance—it was a willingness to engage, reflect, and keep at it. This method is learnable, adaptable, and powerful. And yes, it can work for you, too. You don't have to be perfect to make progress.

MOMENTS OF CLARITY

It can be tough to pull out the main takeaways from a long chapter, especially when you're working to shift how you think in addition to what you know. That's why I've gathered these mindset-shaping highlights from each chapter into moments of insight; these are clear, practical ideas that can help you review the chapter and apply the framework in real life.

- **Build a foundation before making financial decisions.** Don't start with tricks, rules, or shortcuts—start with your decision-making approach. A strong method for making decisions gives every future strategy something solid to stand on.

- **Make intentional choices that reflect your goals.** Align every dollar with your personal values and long-term priorities, not just your short-term wants.

- **Practice, don't perfect.** This method takes time to build. Every decision is a chance to hone your process and improve. The goal is steady improvement rather than perfection.

- **Anyone can do this.** You can develop this method regardless of your background, interests, or personality. I've seen it happen with all kinds of students. It's not about loving finance. It's about being willing to think.

CHAPTER TWO

START WITH A VISION

Picture it: I was a young man, early in my undergraduate studies at Utah State University. While I still had no financial training to speak of, I was quite confident that I was good with money. I worried constantly about my expenses and counted every penny. I scrimped and saved and avoided every purchase I possibly could, no matter what it was.

I've since come to realize that back then, I wasn't as good with money as I believed I was. While my choices weren't necessarily bad, my attitude made me more nervous and stressed than I really needed to be. I could have done the same things with a less stressed and more positive perspective. You see, I wasn't saving as part of a strategy. I didn't have a reason for it. Well, not a *good* reason, anyway. All my financial decisions were driven by the fear of running out of money. That made my life more stressful and painful than it had to be. I could have borrowed just another thousand dollars per year for college and alleviated much of my stress, but my fear of debt held me back.

An extra few thousand dollars of student loan debt would make no appreciable difference in my lifestyle today, but it would have made all the difference to that poor young man who lived in fear of spending his money. My problem back then was that I lacked a vision. I had no motivation, no purpose, no direction for my money other than "don't run out."

That's why the first step in the Strategic Money Method is getting crystal clear about your financial vision. Before you can make smart choices with your money, you need to know what you're aiming for. Without a clear destination, even the most careful budgeting or disciplined saving can feel aimless—or worse, paralyzing. A well-defined vision gives your money a job. It replaces fear with focus and hesitation with intentionality. Your financial vision is a picture of the life you want to live. It's not financial in nature—it's deeply personal. It's about the kind of life you want to build, the experiences you hope to have, and the values you want to uphold. What does your ideal life look like? The clearer this vision is in your mind, the more specifically you can tailor your financial decisions to achieve these dreams.

Imagine your future self. Where are you living? How do you spend your time? Who are you with? What brings you joy? Your financial vision serves as the bedrock for all your financial decisions. Without something you're working toward, your sacrifices and efforts to reach financial success can feel hollow, and you are likely to struggle with motivation.

The vision is your *why*. It provides the purpose and inspiration that fuel your journey, giving meaning to your financial choices and helping you persevere through challenges. This is your personal vision. It could include things like traveling the world, spending time with family, pursuing a passion project, or giving back to your community. It's the foundation for everything else in your financial plan.

By starting with a clear vision, you create a target to aim for. This vision informs every financial choice, helping you prioritize your spending, saving, and investing in ways that align with the life you want to live. In the chapters ahead, we'll explore how to translate this vision into actionable financial goals and strategies; but for now, take the time to dream. The more vivid and detailed your vision, the stronger your foundation for financial success will be.

IDENTIFY YOUR PERSONAL VALUES AND PRIORITIES

To build a meaningful vision, you must start by identifying your personal values and priorities. These are the guiding principles that shape your decisions and define what truly matters to you. Remember that money matters, yes, but only as a means to an end. Money matters because it can become other things, and *those* things have value in your life. Your vision is about identifying those things that matter most. Ask yourself—

- **What do I value most?** This could be relationships, learning, creativity, adventure, health, or making a positive impact on others. Recognizing your core values provides clarity about the foundation of your vision.

- **What are my top priorities?** These are the aspects of life that you want to focus on right now and in the future. Do you want to build strong family relationships, advance in your career, or cultivate a fulfilling hobby?

- **What brings me the most joy and satisfaction?** Reflect on past experiences that have brought you happiness and fulfillment. These insights can guide you toward creating a vision that aligns with what makes you happiest.

By answering these questions, you can uncover the elements of your life that deserve the most attention and resources. Your financial vision should align with these values and priorities to ensure that every financial decision you make supports the life you truly want to build.

ESTABLISH SPECIFIC LIFE GOALS

Once you've identified your personal values and priorities, the next step is to establish specific life goals. These goals can, will, and even should change over time, but your aspirations need to be more concrete than vague dreams. Specific goals give you direction and make it easier to align your financial decisions with your vision.

THESE GOALS SHOULD BE—

- **Specific.** Clearly define what you want to achieve. Instead of saying, "I want to travel," specify, "I want to visit Italy for two weeks next summer."

- **Meaningful.** Ensure that rather than being purely financial, your goals reflect what you genuinely want to achieve personally or socially. Being more specific helps you achieve a goal by making it more concrete and emotionally "real." For example, instead of "Save $10,000," frame it as "Save $10,000 to start my own business." The dream of entrepreneurship makes saving money purposeful, and that purpose can help you push through moments when saving might otherwise feel painful.

- **Aligned with your values.** Your goals should resonate with the values and priorities you've identified. If building strong family relationships is a priority, a goal might be to save for annual family vacations. If you don't truly value what you are trying to accomplish deep down inside, then you will struggle to remain focused and motivated to achieve the goal.

Establishing these life goals creates a road map for your financial journey. They transform abstract aspirations into actionable objectives, providing a sense of purpose and clarity. Remember, these goals are not set in stone—they can evolve as your life circumstances change. Regularly revisiting and refining your goals ensures they remain aligned with your vision and values.

CREATING VISUAL REMINDERS OF YOUR DREAMS

Visual reminders of your dreams can be a powerful tool for staying motivated and focused on your financial vision. Creating a vision board, for example, allows you to collect images, words, and symbols that represent your goals and aspirations. Place this board in a place where you'll see it daily; on your desk, in your bedroom, or even as digital wallpaper. Every glance at it will serve as a reminder of what you're working toward.

Similarly, keeping small tokens or mementos related to your dreams can help you stay inspired. For instance, if your dream is to travel to Italy, keep a postcard or a small figurine of the Colosseum where you'll see it regularly. These visual cues keep your goals at the forefront of your mind and provide a tangible connection to the life you're striving to build.

By incorporating visual reminders into your daily routine, you can strengthen your commitment to your financial vision and maintain the focus needed to achieve your goals. These tools not only inspire, but also provide clarity, helping you stay on track even when distractions or challenges arise.

PICTURE THIS: LIVING YOUR BEST LIFE

You can't focus your spending on what you love most until you know what that is. A great life starts by identifying what truly matters—then building a plan that lets you spend freely on those things without stress.

Visions don't have to be big. Some people feel bad that they don't have "big dreams," but all dreams matter, whether they are big or small. In fact, small dreams tend to be easier to realize and, in that regard, can be more satisfying than big dreams that go unfulfilled. Never be ashamed of your dreams. Regardless of whether your aspirations are to take a local road trip or to climb Mount Everest, what matters most is that you clearly envision the life you want to lead.

Your money should help you realize your dreams, no matter their size. This vision will serve as a motivational tool, providing the inspiration you need to power through the inevitable temptations and trials that will threaten to derail your financial efforts. By staying focused on your personal goals, you'll remain grounded in what truly matters, which will make it easier to navigate the challenges on your path to financial success.

This vision is the cornerstone of all of your financial decisions. You create it by making a careful examination of your wants, needs, goals, priorities, values, and weaknesses. It requires introspection, self-honesty, and a willingness to adjust.

Let's consider an example.

Trevor has always liked the idea of owning a truck. He grew up around them, enjoys outdoor activities, and just likes how they feel to drive. It's not just about utility—there's also an emotional connection. And in his mind, owning a truck would be part of the life he wants to live. To Trevor, trucks are cool, plain and simple.

But when Trevor sat down and created his financial vision, the truck didn't land at the top of the list. It was important, yes, and it ranked highly. But what he discovered was that it mattered more to him to save for a down payment on a house. He wanted a space of his own, something stable and long-term, especially since he was hoping to start a family in the next few years. The house represented security, independence, and a big step toward the life he truly valued.

This is where vision matters. It's not about denying yourself what you want—it's about recognizing what you want *most*. When Trevor is feeling the itch to buy a truck, his vision gives him guidance on how much he should spend to get it. Is the truck worth slowing him down on his path to buying a house? Can he get a less expensive truck that satisfies his desire for the truck while having a lesser impact on his house-buying goal? The vision gives Trevor context and emotional support for his decision to defer the truck.

Trevor will probably still get the truck one day, and there's nothing wrong with that. But by aligning today's choices with his bigger priorities, he puts himself in a stronger position to build the life he really wants. If he doesn't sit down, identify his priorities, and weigh the cost of the truck against the cost of his home-buying dream, then he may spend years spinning his tires; trying to build up enough momentum to buy a house and not realizing that the truck he bought five years ago is holding him back.

DON'T GIVE UP WHAT YOU WANT MOST FOR WHAT YOU WANT NOW.

Your financial vision provides guidance and motivation for how you will spend your money. It establishes the objectives and criteria you'll need in order to build a strategy for how to realize that vision. It's taking a step back and considering which things bring the most utility into your life, then focusing on obtaining those things without wasting money on things that provide little or no utility (even if the thing feels good for a moment).

MOMENTS OF CLARITY

- **Money is a tool, not the goal.** The purpose of money isn't to grow endlessly; it's to help you build the life you want. Use it to pursue joy, security, meaning, and the things that matter most to you.

- **A financial vision gives purpose to your money.** Without a clear vision, your financial decisions may be driven by fear, habit, or vague pressure to "do better." A compelling vision provides motivation, clarity, and direction.

- **Little dreams matter.** Small goals, like more family time or funding a local trip, are just as worthy as grandiose visions, and often more achievable. What matters most is that your vision is authentic to you.

CHAPTER THREE

KEY QUESTION 1: "WHAT'S THE PURPOSE OF THE PURCHASE?"

When I think about the purpose of money, I'm reminded of Reggie, a friend from college. Reggie landed what most of us considered the dream job right out of school—a high-paying position at a prestigious financial firm. From the outside, it seemed like he had it all: a luxury apartment downtown, a shiny new car, and the kind of paycheck that could make anyone jealous. But after only a year, Reggie shocked everyone by quitting. He was living the dream and he just walked away? Madness.

When I asked him why, he said something I'll never forget: "I realized I was spending all this money just to survive the stress of my job. Fancy dinners, expensive vacations, new gadgets—none of it made me happy. It just helped me cope." The long hours, constant travel, and unrelenting pressure had drained him. Reggie's lifestyle had become a way to distract himself from how miserable he felt. The high-paying job that was supposed to make his life better was actually making it worse, and no amount of money could fix it.

THE PURPOSE OF THE PURCHASE

Good financial management isn't about making or keeping money for its own sake. In fact, focusing too much on money can lead to decisions that cause heartache and misery. The ultimate goal of financial planning isn't to accumulate wealth—it's to maximize happiness and well-being over your lifetime.

Reggie's experience is a perfect example of what happens when we lose sight of money's true purpose: to make our lives better, not worse. He, like so many of us in our graduating class, thought that making more money would make him happier. In reality, his happiness depended on far more than just how much money he made. Money is just one resource among many that we use to improve our lives.

In this context, a resource is anything we use to improve our lives. We all have limited resources, whether we're talking about time, energy, or money. Even the wealthiest individuals face limits on what they can access and use. This is the principle of scarcity. Because of scarcity, we can't have everything we want from life, so we have to carefully choose how to allocate our resources. Good financial management is about making these choices in a way that brings the most value and joy to your life.

This is why the first of the three key questions to ask when facing a financial decision is about the function of the purchase. At its core, we want every purchase to serve at least two purposes. The first is to contribute to our ability to realize our long-term goals as outlined in our vision. The second is to meet the needs of the moment.

So much of what we buy doesn't actually improve our lives. We spend and spend, hoping the purchases will make us happier, but they usually don't. A new gadget, designer clothes, the latest kitchen appliance, or even a luxury car might feel exciting at first, but the satisfaction often fades fast. These short-term purchases may meet a momentary want or soothe a passing discomfort, but they often do so at the expense of our long-term goals. When we're not careful, we trade enduring progress towards what we want most out of life for fleeting pleasures of the moment. When you stay focused on what you're trying to accomplish with each purchase, and on how it might improve your level of happiness, you're more likely to use your money in ways that truly add value, instead of trading your well-being for clutter that doesn't satisfy.

Understanding the purpose behind each purchase is a great idea, but to identify the purpose you need to first be able to answer a much deeper question: *What actually makes me happy?* To spend with intention, we need to know what kinds of spending truly bring satisfaction. Each individual is going to have a different answer to that question. However, there are general trends and patterns that we can observe that can help us as we examine our own lives for areas of spending that are *not* bringing satisfaction. That's where the research comes in. Science offers powerful insights into how money connects to happiness—and it often reveals that our instincts can lead us astray.

THE LINK BETWEEN MONEY AND HAPPINESS

The relationship between money and happiness has been a subject of debate for thousands of years. Philosophers have long argued over whether money can buy happiness. Some say the best things in life are free, while others argue that money's ability to provide comfort, pleasure, and opportunity makes it essential to happiness.

Economists have joined this discussion in recent decades, using surveys and scientific tools to explore how money impacts happiness. Their findings are fascinating and provide practical insights for managing your resources.

Economists often use the term *utility* to describe the ways in which goods and services improve our lives. Utility includes feelings of happiness, comfort, satisfaction, and reduced stress. For example, a car provides utility by offering transportation, but it might also make someone happy because they find it beautiful. On the other hand, a purchase that isn't used—like an expensive outfit you're afraid to wear—provides little to no utility. Thinking critically about the utility a purchase will bring to your life can help you make better financial decisions.

The following are some key insights about money and happiness.

WHAT MONEY CAN'T BUY

One of the most intriguing studies on the connection between income and happiness was conducted by Daniel Kahneman, Matthew Killingsworth, and Barbara Mellers in 2023.[1] Their research sheds light on the complex ways income influences well-being. The study found that, on average, happiness increases with income, but the relationship

---

1   Matthew A. Killingsworth, Daniel Kahneman, and Barbara Mellers, "Income and Emotional Well-Being: A Conflict Resolved," *Proceedings of the National Academy of Sciences* 120, no. 10 (2023): e2208661120, https://doi.org/10.1073/pnas.2208661120.

isn't straightforward; sure, happiness increases with income, but the more money you earn, the less of an impact each extra dollar has on your overall happiness.

Interestingly, the researchers discovered that the impact of income on happiness varies depending on an individual's baseline level of emotional well-being. For the least happy individuals, higher income does improve happiness, but only up to a certain threshold. Beyond that point, additional income has little effect on reducing unhappiness. In contrast, for people who are already relatively happy, income continues to enhance happiness without a clear plateau. In fact, for the happiest individuals, the relationship between income and well-being even accelerates at higher income levels.

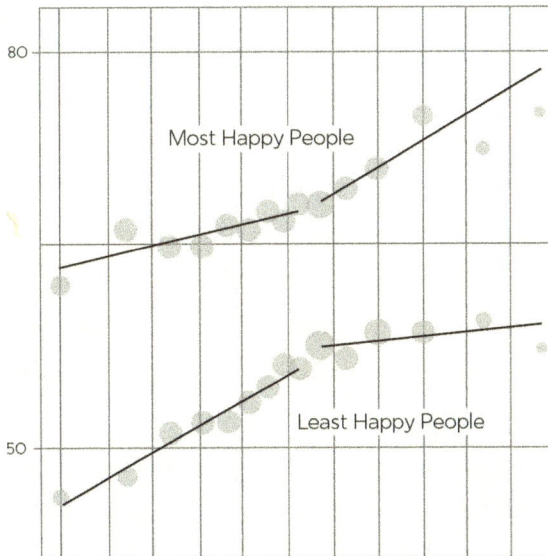

FIGURE 3.1. Happiness versus income by inherent level of happiness. Adapted from Kahneman, Killingsworth, and Mellers, 2023

This research underscores two important takeaways.

First, for individuals experiencing low levels of happiness, increasing income can lead to meaningful improvements in well-being, but only up to a point. Beyond that, other factors, like relationships, health, and personal fulfillment, become more significant contributors to happiness. This implies that money can alleviate some of life's stresses, fears, and pains; but not all of them, and only up to a certain point. If you are unhappy in life, please keep in mind that while accumulating or spending more money might give some fleeting moments of relief, there is nothing you can buy that will mend your heartache, soothe your grief, fix your relationships, or improve your job satisfaction. Trying to fill such painful voids with spending will only create additional problems by increasing your financial distress.

Second, money and the things it buys can enhance the good things in your life, but most of the benefit it provides comes from providing stability and security. Most of the change in happiness comes in the lower levels of income, even for the groups whose happiness increased with high income. This suggests that the luxuries of high income are not the most important expenses to protect. Rather, it's the basic knowledge that you can afford rent and groceries this month, that your kids can join the soccer team or take dance lessons, that bring the most joy for the fewest dollars. In other words, it is not essential to have high income or be an "inherently happy" person to benefit from the joys that money can buy. Many people are quite happy to make enough income to buy security, and then to use their additional time and talent pursuing the joys that money cannot buy.

While money can improve your circumstances, it's not a cure-all for unhappiness. If you're deeply dissatisfied with your life, simply earning more won't solve underlying issues. True happiness comes from within—from relationships, purpose, and personal growth. Financial security can enhance your well-being, but it's most effective when paired with a fulfilling inner life.

STOP COMPARING YOURSELF TO OTHERS

One of the main reasons increasing income doesn't usually lead to increasing happiness is because there is always someone who has more. Humans are social creatures; we love to compare ourselves to others. We love to have more than others, and we hate having less.

At first glance, it seems obvious: More money should mean more happiness. And on an individual level, that's often true—higher income can improve quality of life, reduce stress, and open up opportunities. That's exactly what we just saw in the Kahneman, Killingworth, and Mellers chart earlier in this chapter. Overall, more money means more happiness.

But when we zoom out and look at entire countries over time, the story gets more complicated.

The following chart shows that as the average income of a country increases, the percentage of people who report being very happy does not increase. How can this be? How is it possible for income to increase happiness in one study, but not in another? This contradictory evidence is the foundation of an economic puzzle called the Easterlin Paradox.

The answer is complicated and took decades of research to conclusively prove, but comparisons appear to be the main reason. As a country gets richer, you might expect everyone would get happier too—but that's not always how it works. Sure, when the economy grows, most people tend to earn more over time, even if some groups get a bigger slice of the pie than others. But here's the strange thing: Even as incomes go up, happiness doesn't always follow. Why? Because we don't just care about how much we have—we also care about how we stack up against others. If your neighbor gets a raise, buys a new car, and goes on a fancy

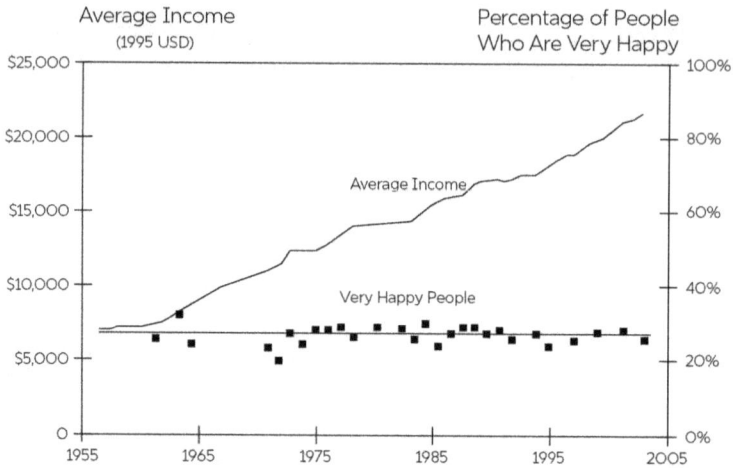

FIGURE 3.2. The Easterlin Paradox: A nation's happiness does not keep up with its income. Adapted from David G. Myers, *The American Paradox*, 2000

vacation, it can make your own progress feel small, even if you're doing better than you were five years ago. Thus the "happiness" we feel by having more income in total is actually balanced by the dissatisfaction of comparing ourselves to our neighbors, who also have more.[2]

Even before social media, people often presented curated versions of their lives to the world; highlighting the wins, hiding the losses. Someone pulling up in a luxury car or wearing designer clothes might seem confident and prosperous, but behind the scenes, they could be juggling credit card debt, living paycheck to paycheck, or feeling anxious about their financial future.

Why the disconnect? Because humans are social creatures wired to seek approval and status. We like to signal success: not just to feel

---

2   Felix Cheung and Richard E. Lucas, "Income Inequality Is Associated with Stronger Social Comparison Effects: The Effect of Relative Income on Life Satisfaction," *Journal of Personality and Social Psychology* 110, no. 2 (2016): 332–341, https://doi.org/10.1037/pspp0000059.

good about ourselves, but to gain respect, admiration, or even envy from others. Psychologists call this *impression management*—our tendency to want to shape how others perceive us. Financially, that often means spending in ways that project wealth rather than build it.

In the mid-20th century, most American families lived in smaller homes with fewer amenities than we consider standard today. The most basic modern car is faster, safer, and comes with more features than the most luxurious vehicle from fifty years ago. Yet despite all this material progress, overall happiness has barely budged. It turns out that once our basic needs are met, more square footage, fancier gadgets, or larger wardrobes don't guarantee more joy, they just raise the bar for what we think we *should* have.

It's no accident that there are no 1,900-square-foot homes in a neighborhood of 10,000-square-foot mansions. No one wants to have the smallest house on the block, surrounded by homes that make theirs feel modest or inadequate. Even if it's spacious by any reasonable standard, living next to vastly larger homes can make people feel like they're falling short. But place that exact same 1,900-square-foot home in a neighborhood of 900-square-foot houses, and suddenly it feels grand. It's the envy of the block: the big house, the extra space, the nice driveway. Nothing about the house changed, but everything about how it *feels* did. This is the power of relative status, and it shows how much our satisfaction depends not just on what we have, but on how it compares to what others have.

This desire to keep up with our friends, family, and neighbors drives many to spend beyond their means. It's not new, and it's not just scoring likes on TikTok. It's a deep-rooted part of human behavior: trying to belong, to compete, to matter. But appearances can be deceiving, and the cost of keeping up with others often includes private stress, debt, and financial fragility.

THE *APPEARANCE* OF SUCCESS RARELY CORRESPONDS TO HOW WELL PEOPLE ARE ACTUALLY DOING.

Stop comparing yourself to others and instead compare your current situation to your past self. Are you doing better than before? Then great, celebrate that! Are you doing worse? Then buckle down and try to improve the situation.

I recognize that this is easier said than done. I am not perfect at this myself. Comparing is a natural part of our human instinct. But as much as you can, please try to let go of this harmful habit. The more you do, the happier you will be.[3]

AVOID THE TRAP OF SNAP SPENDING

Ever grabbed something off the shelf just because it *looked* right? Or added something to your cart without a second thought because the price seemed too good to pass up? That's what I like to call *snap spending*: quick, instinctive purchases made in the moment, often without much thought about whether they fit your budget, your goals, or even your real needs.

Everybody engages in snap spending to some degree. It's just the way human brains are wired to work. Even I have moments of snap spending, where I buy on impulse or based on my current emotions or mood.

However, people who rely too much on snap spending inevitably wind up spending a lot of money on things that don't genuinely improve their lives, or that do so only fleetingly. The thrill of a new purchase often fades quickly, leaving us with clutter and regret. That regret in turn leads us to spend more, to seek out and renew the spike of pleasure the last

---

3 Mariano Rojas, "Affluence: More Relative Than Absolute," in *Wealth(s) and Subjective Well-Being* (Springer, 2019), 147–166.

purchase provided. Before we know it, this kind of emotional, reflexive snap-spending decision leads us into a spiral of endless spending that brings no real improvement in our levels of happiness or life satisfaction.

Snap spending is powered by what psychologists call System 1 thinking[4]—your brain's fast, automatic, emotional response system. It's the system of mental shortcuts that helps you survive in a world full of choices by reacting quickly instead of weighing every pro and con.

System 1 is easy. It's effortless, automatic, and—honestly—kind of nice to rely on. It's our default mode of thinking, the part of the brain that goes with gut instinct, emotion, and habit. When you make a purchase because it *feels right* in the moment, or because you're just reacting to a sale, a craving, or a mood—that's System 1 in action. And because it doesn't require any heavy thinking, it feels painless. No mental strain, no inner debate. Just act, spend, enjoy the moment, and move on. Your mind's System 1 processes make decisions feel fast and effortless—like a snap. That's why I call it snap spending.

But that ease comes at a cost.

System 1 doesn't pause to weigh the future benefits of your choices. It doesn't care whether something aligns with your personal values or long-term goals. It's not interested in building wealth or security. It wants to satisfy whatever you're feeling *right now*—boredom, stress, excitement, hunger, envy. So when System 1 is driving your financial decisions, you're not building a strong foundation. You're chasing quick hits of satisfaction, moment to moment, without asking the bigger questions: *Will this actually improve my life? Does this purchase support the kind of future I want?*

Spending from this place rarely leads to lasting fulfillment. It leads to clutter, financial stress, and the nagging sense that you're working hard

---

4   Daniel Kahneman, *Thinking, Fast and Slow* (Farrar, Straus and Giroux, 2011).

but not getting ahead. That's why building a stronger financial mindset starts with learning to recognize when System 1 is taking over, and choosing, even just occasionally, to hit pause and think a little deeper.

When we're in snap-spending mode, we're especially vulnerable to things like ads, popular trends, moods, sales pitches, and even just seeing someone else's shiny new toy. It all feels natural in the moment—but that's the problem. These fast, intuitive decisions often bypass the slower, more deliberate thought process that would ask, *Do I actually need this?* or *Is this helping me reach my goals?*

Jenna's Snap Spending

One of my students once shared a story with me that stuck. Let's call her Jenna.

Jenna told me she never thought of herself as someone who had a problem with spending. She wasn't into designer labels or maxing out credit cards. But after we talked about focusing on function and the dangers of snap spending in class, something clicked. She realized that even though her purchases were small—candles, water bottles, wellness kits—there was a pattern. A feeling she was chasing.

It always started the same way: a hard day, a little stress, a sense that something was missing. Then came the click—*Buy Now*—and for a moment, it felt like she was doing something good for herself. A fix. A fresh start.

But that positive feeling faded fast every single time. The candle burned out. The water bottle got shoved into a cabinet with the others. The speaker sat unused. And yet the spending kept happening, not because she needed the things, but because it felt easier than facing the discomfort underneath.

Then, she told me, one night it finally sank in. She paused, her thumb over the *Buy* button, and it hit her. In that moment, Jenna finally saw the pattern for what it was. She'd been trying to purchase peace of mind. But Amazon doesn't deliver that! So, for the first time in a long time, she backed out of the cart without hitting buy.

It didn't feel great—no dopamine rush, no instant satisfaction—but it felt *different*. Like she was finally starting to take the wheel.

"I'm not perfect," she said. "But at least now I'm thinking. I'm asking myself what I actually need—and what I'm trying to feel. That's new for me."

That's the kind of shift we're aiming for. Not perfection. Just awareness, intention, and one better decision at a time.

HITTING THE PAUSE BUTTON BRINGS CLARITY

At the most basic level, every financial decision shares one broad function: to make our lives better and bring us some measure of happiness. But that's not enough. Each individual decision should also serve a more specific objective, one that fits the situation and reflects what you truly need in that moment.

System 1 thinking, though—that quick, emotional, gut-driven reaction—doesn't stop to ask what function a purchase serves. It just chases whatever feels good right now. That's how you end up buying a $70 hoodie when what you really needed was a night to decompress. Or end up grabbing takeout every day, not because you're hungry, but because you're overwhelmed and craving comfort.

Focusing on function helps interrupt that cycle. It gives you a pause button. It encourages you to ask, *What am I really trying to achieve with this money?* Maybe it's nourishment, not just convenience. Maybe it's confidence for a job interview, not just another pair of shoes.

In every case, identifying the true purpose of a purchase brings clarity, and that clarity makes it much easier to choose options that actually serve you. We'll dive deeper into that idea when we get to Key Question #2: Is It Worth the Cost? There, we'll explore how to make sure each purchase meets its intended function without sacrificing long-term well-being.

BALANCE RESOURCES FOR A LIFETIME

It's easy to get caught up in the *now*. The paycheck hits, the weekend plans roll in, and your money feels like it's already spoken for. But here's the thing: you're not just living for today. You're also living for tomorrow . . . and next year . . . and for decades down the line.

Financial security doesn't come from making perfect choices, it comes from making *balanced* ones. That means learning to manage your money not just for the short term, but for your whole life. Think of it like rationing supplies on a long road trip: If you burn through everything in the first few miles, you're going to be stranded before the journey's done.

Imagine you win a prize: fifty all-expenses-paid vacations. Sounds amazing, right? But here's the catch—you have to take all fifty trips this year. That's nearly one per week.

At first, it's thrilling. The beach, the mountains, the city lights—it's a dream come true. But by vacation number twelve, you're jet-lagged, living out of a suitcase, and starting to feel like every new destination looks the same. By vacation number thirty, you're checking your phone more than the scenery. The magic wears off. The joy fades.

Now imagine spreading those fifty vacations over fifty years. One trip a year. Each one a break from routine, something to anticipate and remember. The excitement is renewed every time, and the enjoyment stays high.

This illustrates a principle that economists call *diminishing marginal utility*—the more you consume something in a short period, the less satisfaction each additional unit brings. The first dollars you spend—on food, shelter, basic needs—bring huge value. They literally keep you alive and well. The next dollars go toward comfort, then convenience, then fun. But eventually you're spending on upgrades that don't add much to your happiness: a slightly nicer phone, a fancier version of something you already own. The utility per dollar is shrinking.

SPEND SMART AND GET JUST AS MUCH JOY

This principle is crucial when planning for your financial future. Spending heavily now can feel good short-term, but each purchase delivers less and less joy. Spreading your spending across time—especially into future periods where your needs might be higher or income might be lower—helps you get *more total utility* from the same amount of money.

You can achieve this steady standard of living by borrowing and saving. Borrowing is simply the process by which we transfer future income into the present so that we can spend it. Saving is the reverse; it is the process by which we transfer money from the present into the future so that we can spend it later. Later in the book, we will discuss these two processes extensively, and how to implement a method that leverages them without causing harm. For now, simply keep in mind that borrowing and saving are simply tools for empowering a more consistent, and therefore more satisfying, lifestyle; not just today, but across your whole life.

Ultimately, the goal of financial management is not to amass wealth for its own sake but to use your resources in ways that bring you the greatest joy, stability, and fulfillment. By understanding the relationship between money and happiness, and by focusing on spending in ways that align with your values, you can create a financial plan that enhances your overall well-being and gives you the happiest life that your money can buy.

So how much happiness can money buy? The answer to that question will likely remain different for everyone. For some it can buy a little, for others it can buy a lot. The amount of happiness money can buy for you doesn't change the main point. We want as much as we can get of whatever positive impact money can have on our lives. But for you, the positive effects might be different than for me. That's why so much generic financial advice winds up being useless at best, and harmful at worst for so many people.

Everyone will have a different definition of success, because everyone derives joy in different ways. Happiness isn't something you get or buy. It is something you cultivate. And money, when managed wisely, can be a powerful tool in that process of cultivation. That's why in the next chapter, we'll dig into how "wise management" isn't a one-size-fits-all formula, but a deeply personal process shaped by your own values and goals, and your own vision for a meaningful life.

MOMENTS OF CLARITY

- **Money is a tool, not the goal.** The purpose of financial planning isn't to accumulate wealth—it's to use your resources to improve your life, happiness, and overall well-being.

- **Focus on function.** Spend your money on things that align with your values, your needs, and your vision for a meaningful life; not what's trendy or what might make you feel better only momentarily. In the end, financial success isn't about how much you have—it's about how well your spending supports the life you actually want to live.

- **Snap spending steals joy.** System 1 thinking leads to quick, emotional purchases that often disappoint. Lasting satisfaction comes from intentional, values-aligned spending. Noticing your emotional triggers and hitting pause—even briefly—can shift you from snap spending to deliberate spending.

- **Balance over time.** Financial planning is a lifelong game. Avoid front-loading your spending; spread it out to maximize satisfaction through every stage of life.

- **Stop comparing yourself to others.** Happiness isn't about having the most, it's about having enough. The more you measure your life against someone else's, the harder it is to appreciate your own.

CHAPTER FOUR

KEY QUESTION 2: "IS IT WORTH THE COST?"

A while back, my wife and I were on a trip with some friends. We were staying at a hotel that didn't offer free breakfast, but it did have a minifridge in the room. So before checking in, we made a quick stop at a grocery store and picked up a bag of bagels, a tub of cream cheese, and some fruit—our go-to travel breakfast setup.

Our friends rolled their eyes. "Really? Bagels in the hotel room?" Yep. Really.

Here's the thing: I love a good eggs Benedict. Bring on the pancakes, donuts, and other breakfast goodies. I'm a huge fan of breakfast. But let's do the math. Breakfast at a café runs about $10 a person. For a four-day trip, that's $80 for just the two of us on breakfast alone. Meanwhile, we spent $8 on our bagel setup. That's $72 saved right there.

And that $72? That's a boat tour. Or a ferry ride. Or museum tickets. It's another layer of memory-making that we get to say yes to because we said no to overpriced morning hash browns. We're not skipping breakfast to be miserable—we're doing it so we can enjoy the trip more without stressing about money when we get home.

People sometimes think we're being cheap. That's fine. We don't mind being called cheap about breakfast if it helps us afford richer experiences throughout the day, and a more secure future long after the trip ends. For us, it's not about deprivation. It's about alignment. We know what matters most to us, and waffles just aren't on the list.

ONE MAN'S TRASH . . .

You probably think about money very differently than I do. You also probably spend very differently than I do. That's not only permissible; it's good! You shouldn't try to copy me, nor should I try to copy you. Money is deeply personal. It is so personal that surveys have found that most people would prefer to discuss their sex lives over talking about money.[5] Even psychiatrists are sometimes hesitant to ask their patients about their finances. One paper put it this way: "Ironically, the first reaction of many child and adolescent psychiatrists discussing a case may be that asking about money in the family feels 'too personal.'"[6]

No two people think about, use, or derive satisfaction from money in exactly the same way. Some people find joy in spending on experiences: traveling to new places, going to concerts, or sharing meals with friends. For them, memories and connection matter more than material things.

---

5   *Money Habits & Confessions Survey* (LearnVest, 2016).

6   Michael S. Jellinek and Eugene Beresin, "Money Talks: Becoming More Comfortable with Understanding a Family's Finances," *Journal of the American Academy of Child & Adolescent Psychiatry* 47, no. 3 (2008): 249–253, https://doi.org/10.1097/CHI.0B013E3181619858.

Others prioritize saving for future security. They feel most at peace when they see their retirement accounts grow or know they can cover unexpected expenses without worry.

Some thrive on the freedom that comes with financial independence. They value the ability to walk away from a job, take a sabbatical, or pursue a passion project without relying on a paycheck. Others feel a deep sense of satisfaction from being prepared—having a stocked pantry, a well-maintained car, or the knowledge that their family is protected by insurance and an emergency fund.

For one person, joy might come from investing in their education or building a business. For another, it could be upgrading their home to create a cozy, welcoming space. Some find happiness in giving, whether through charitable donations, supporting a friend in need, or spoiling their grandkids. Others light up when they can spend on hobbies, pets, fitness, art, or gear for weekend adventures.

There's no one-size-fits-all answer. The point is to know what *you* care about, and then make financial choices that reflect and support that. Because when your spending aligns with your values, money becomes a tool for fulfillment, not a source of stress or regret.

This book is not about telling you what you should or should not buy. Instead, it's about helping you understand your own relationship with money: what you value most, what brings you satisfaction, and how you can align your financial decisions with your unique needs and desires. By embracing your individuality, you'll be able to craft a plan that supports your goals and enhances your life.

YOUR RELATIONSHIP WITH MONEY

When it comes to financial decisions, there are no universal right answers. What works for one person might not work for another, and that's okay. That's why the second key question in our strategic money method is: *How does the cost compare to the benefits?* Asking this question will allow us to figure out whether the purchase is worth the cost.

Weighing costs and benefits is not about finding a single correct solution; it's about finding the best choice for you, given your unique circumstances, values, and goals. That's the secret to this second key question of the money method.

> YOU ARE ALLOWED TO BUY EXPENSIVE
> THINGS SO LONG AS THEY PROVIDE
> SIMILARLY LARGE BENEFITS.

This process requires balancing tangible factors with intangible ones, many of which are emotional and personal. And yes, you *can* put a price on intangibles. In fact, you *must* put a price on them.

So how do we do that? How do we stop and identify whether a purchase is worth it? Start with the easy part: the cost.

IDENTIFY THE COSTS

Cost is rarely just the number on the price tag. There are often a variety of other costs, both financial and intangible, to consider. If you use a loan to make a purchase, then you must also consider the cost of the loan—interest payments, fees, and any financial constraints the loan places on you. Beyond that, it's helpful to think about cost in terms of trade-offs. For example, if you spend $10 on a fast food meal, what else could you have bought for $10? Would something else have improved your life more than a burger and fries?

Every purchase affects not just today, but your future as well. A dollar spent today is a dollar you cannot spend tomorrow; and if it could have been saved or invested to grow over time, it may even be worth more than a dollar in the future. Financial decisions are interconnected—what you chose to do with your money yesterday determines your financial opportunities today, and the choices you make now will shape the options available to you in the future.

Take James, for example. James lives in the moment. He loves treating himself, whether it's grabbing takeout, buying the latest gadget, or booking spontaneous weekend trips. But while the spending feels good in the short term, over time James has built up a mountain of credit card debt and has no savings to fall back on. When his car breaks down or a medical bill pops up, he's forced to borrow more just to stay afloat. Spending all his money on making today as good as possible means he has no flexibility or security in the future. The stress adds up, and so do the interest payments.

Then there's Brandi. Brandi's the opposite—disciplined to a fault. She saves diligently, avoids unnecessary expenses, and always pays her bills on time. She has a growing emergency fund and feels secure knowing she can handle whatever life throws at her. But there's a flip side: Brandi rarely lets herself enjoy the money she's worked so hard to earn. She skips outings with friends, avoids hobbies she loves, and turns down travel opportunities, even when she can afford them, because she's afraid of spending. She has security in the future but is not living her life as fully as she might if she could let herself use her money.

Neither James nor Brandi has found an ideal balance yet. James is focused only on the benefits of spending, while Brandi thinks almost exclusively about costs. Together, their stories highlight the principle: When you consistently spend without saving, you limit your future options and increase your vulnerability. And when you save without allowing any room for enjoyment, you may miss out on the very happiness that money is meant to support. The goal is thoughtful spending:

making choices that align with both your present needs and your long-term well-being.

IDENTIFY THE BENEFITS

When weighing a financial decision, it's just as important to identify the benefits as it is to recognize the costs. Benefits can be financial, such as saving money on interest by paying off debt early, or they can be intangible, like the peace of mind that comes from knowing you have an emergency fund. Unlike costs, which are often straightforward to calculate, benefits are much harder to quantify because they are largely intangible.

For example, accumulating a savings fund eliminates the cost of taking on debt in the future. Suppose you set aside $200 per month in an emergency fund instead of spending it on unnecessary wants. Over time, this fund grows, and when an unexpected expense arises, like a car repair or a medical bill, you can pay for it without relying on high-interest credit cards or loans. The benefit here is not just the ability to cover an expense but also avoiding the added cost of interest and the stress of added debt. However, these benefits are often overlooked because they do not come with a clear price tag the way costs do.

FOCUS ON FUNCTION

Identifying benefits is closely tied to understanding the purpose of a purchase. Once you determine the wants and needs a purchase is fulfilling, you can better assess its value to you. This is why our first key question is to ask yourself about the purpose of the purchase, and the second is to ask if meeting that purpose is worth the cost.

When you recognize what you are truly trying to accomplish with a purchase, you can better evaluate whether the benefits justify the costs. Some benefits are immediate and tangible, such as a reliable car that gets you to work every day. Others are intangible, like the peace of mind that comes with financial security, or the sense of fulfillment from a meaningful experience. Understanding both the practical and emotional benefits of a purchase helps ensure that your spending aligns with what genuinely improves your life.

I love *Star Wars*. The sights, sounds, colors, and imagery just make me happy. So it might come as no surprise that I wanted a nice, high-quality lightsaber toy for a long time. I just thought it would be fun and cool. Problem is, the cheapest ones were many hundreds of dollars, and some were thousands of dollars.

When I evaluated the benefits, I realize that my only benefit was the enjoyment of looking at it. While I would enjoy how cool it was, I knew that it likely would just sit on a shelf or hang from the wall, and I would rarely if ever actually turn it on. And if I'm not going to turn it on and use it, then it felt rather pointless to me. I decided that I couldn't spend hundreds of dollars on what would ultimately amount to a simple decoration. It just wasn't worth it. The costs were high and the benefits were negligible and fleeting.

THE PRICE OF INTANGIBLES

We like to say, "You can't put a price on that smile," or "You can't put a price on happiness." I beg to differ. While it's true that money cannot convey the true value of smiles or happiness, you can decide how much these things are worth to you. Not only *can* you put a price on these things, but you *must* if you want to make thoughtful financial decisions. In fact, I'd wager that every one of us does this every single day even if we don't realize it.

Take the example of a family trip to Disney World. Some might argue that you can't put a price on the joy your children will experience, but the truth is, you already are. If you couldn't price joy, then everyone who loves Disney World would be there all the time. Every bride would have a designer wedding dress. Santa would bring every child every item on their Christmas list. I would have a den full of expensive *Star Wars* toys (I'm looking at you, Lego Death Star II!).

Instead, we each have decided to limit how much we spend on even the most valuable things. Every financial decision has a point where we say, "I will spend no more on this." That's the price. It's not an easy calculation, because emotions and feelings don't translate directly into dollars, and circumstances play a significant role in these decisions. Our emotional awareness, values, and priorities shape how we weigh the trade-offs.

The simple fact is that you decide the price of happiness every single day. You probably just don't realize it. When you drive past McDonald's in order to save money, you are deciding that the happiness of a Happy Meal is less than what it costs, at least in that moment. When you pick the expensive name-brand breakfast cereal, you are deciding that the pleasure of the more expensive cereal is worth the higher cost.

It's easy to make decisions subconsciously and without deliberate thought. It's the default human method of operating. That's why it's important to remember to deliberately pause in the decision-making process when making significant choices. Making significant financial decisions by reflex or instinct generally results in spending money on momentary whims every time we feel in any way stressed, sad, tired, or unhappy. This, in turn, leads us to run in circles, spending endlessly but never finding peace or happiness, like my student Jenna reported.

This habit of spending in fruitless circles has actually been scientifically studied. Economic and psychological researchers have aptly named it the "hedonic treadmill."[7] Hedonic refers to the pursuit of physical pleasures, and a treadmill is a device that makes you work but takes you nowhere. The hedonic treadmill is the idea that no matter how much your circumstances improve—more money, nicer stuff, better lifestyle—you tend to return to a stable level of happiness over time. That new car smell fades, the excitement of a bigger house wears off, and even the thrill of a dream vacation becomes just another memory.

This doesn't mean happiness isn't real or that joy from purchases is meaningless, but it does mean that chasing happiness through ever-increasing consumption is a losing game. If we're not careful, we can find ourselves sprinting on this treadmill: spending more and more only to end up no happier than when we started. The key is stepping off the treadmill and aligning spending with true, lasting sources of satisfaction.

The best way to do this is to take the time to reflect on what function each decision serves, what need it will meet, and what wants it will fulfill. This deliberate reflection ensures that your choices align with your goals and provide maximum satisfaction for the resources spent.

Weighing costs and benefits involves more than adding up the dollar amount of a purchase. Tangible costs, such as the price tag of a car or the interest on a loan, are usually straightforward to calculate. Online tools and calculators can help you compare options and see the financial impact of your decisions.

---

7   Philip Brickman and Donald T. Campbell, "Hedonic Relativism and Planning the Good Society," in *Adaptation-Level Theory: A Symposium*, ed. Mortimer H. Appley (Academic Press, 1971), 287–302; Ed Diener, Richard E. Lucas, and Christie Napa Scollon, "Beyond the Hedonic Treadmill: Revising the Adaptation Theory of Well-Being," *American Psychologist* 61, no. 4 (2006): 305–314.

CONSIDER THE INTANGIBLES

The real challenge comes with intangible costs and benefits. For example—

- How much is the convenience of living closer to work worth to you?

- How much do you value the experience of dining out versus cooking at home?

- How do you measure the peace of mind that comes with having an emergency fund?

These intangibles are harder to quantify, but they matter just as much as the dollars and cents. What brings one person joy might not do the same for someone else—and that's the point.

Remember Spendy James from before? Despite the sometimes harsh negative effects of his impulsive spending habits, there's one thing he never regrets: taking his kids to Disney World. He lights up when he talks about it—the laughter, the bonding, the once-in-a-lifetime memories. For James, that trip, even with its high price tag, felt completely worth it. It brought a level of joy and connection that no spreadsheet could capture. Not having an emergency fund is stressful, but at least he has the memories.

Brandi, on the other hand, wouldn't touch a Disney trip with a ten-foot budget pole. To her, that kind of expense feels overwhelming and wasteful. But redoing the backyard so her family can grill out, play games, and unwind together every weekend? That's money well spent for her. It brings her a sense of peace and comfort that aligns with her values and lifestyle. She particularly likes that she can enjoy the back yard for years and years to come, rather than for just the length of a Disney trip. And it will hopefully increase the value of her home if she ever needs to sell it.

Neither approach is right or wrong. What matters is knowing

yourself—what truly brings *you* joy, fulfillment, and peace—and aligning your spending with that. Whether it's adventure, comfort, connection, or beauty, spending intentionally on the things that matter most will always bring the highest return.

COMPARE AND REFLECT

Once you've identified the costs and benefits, step back and reflect. Does the benefit justify the cost? Are there other ways to achieve the same benefit for less? Are you being honest about what really matters to you?

Because financial decisions often involve emotions, they can feel overwhelming. Guilt, fear, and excitement can cloud our judgment. Recognizing this emotional component doesn't mean dismissing it; rather, it's about understanding and integrating it into your decision-making process.

For example, if you're planning a vacation, you might feel guilty about spending money. But if that trip fulfills your need for connection, relaxation, or adventure, it might be worth every penny. The key is to acknowledge those feelings, weigh them against the tangible costs, and decide whether the purchase aligns with your values and goals.

Weighing costs and benefits is a deeply personal process, and there's no formula for getting it right every time. What matters is that you're intentional and thoughtful about your decisions. This process helps you avoid spending a lot for fleeting or trivial emotional gains, and instead focus your money on the things that bring the most joy and pleasure for the longest time with the least amount of money. By considering both the tangible and intangible factors, and by putting a price on the things that matter most to you, you'll be able to make financial choices that support your well-being and move you closer to your goals.

MOMENTS OF CLARITY

- **Financial choices are personal, not universal.** What's worth it to one person might be wasteful to another. The key is understanding your own values, emotions, and priorities.

- **You *can* put a price on happiness.** Every day, you decide what joy is worth, whether by skipping a Happy Meal or splurging on a vacation. Just do it consciously.

- **Function first, emotion second.** Ask: *What is this purchase really doing for me? What need or want is it fulfilling? How much am I really willing to spend on this?*

- **Every purchase has more than one cost.** Costs include trade-offs, future limitations, interest, stress, and lost opportunities—not just price tags.

CHAPTER FIVE

KEY QUESTION 3: "IS THERE A SMART SWAP?"

Identifying your needs is essential when making financial decisions. In our earlier discussions, we emphasized the importance of understanding what you're truly trying to buy. This awareness helps ensure that your spending aligns with your goals and values. However, identifying your needs serves another critical purpose: It empowers you to recognize that there may be less expensive ways to meet those needs. By exploring alternatives, you can stretch your resources further and create more value for your money.

What we think we're buying is often different from what we're actually purchasing. For example, you might think you're buying a truck, but in reality, you're buying transportation. You might think you're buying food at a restaurant, but you're really paying for convenience or time with friends. These intangible benefits—convenience, recognition, entertainment—are fine things to spend money on, but it's essential to be clear about what you're really buying. This clarity allows you to decide if you're overpaying for these intangible benefits, and it empowers you to explore alternative ways to meet your needs at a lower cost.

NEEDS AND WANTS: THE FOUNDATION OF MINDFUL SPENDING

Understanding your relationship with money begins with identifying your needs and wants.

I've heard a lot of definitions of need, but the one I like best is one I first heard proposed by Dr. Sarah Newcomb. She defines a need as something that every single person on the planet must have to survive. This includes essentials like nutrition, shelter, transportation, rest, love, and time. Everything else is a want.

This distinction isn't about judgment; it's about clarity. Needs are nonnegotiable, but they don't have to be expensive. By carefully evaluating your real needs, you can often find ways to meet them for less, freeing up resources for the wants that truly make your life better. For example, transportation is a need, but a luxury SUV might be a want. If your primary goal is getting from point A to point B, a smaller car, public transit, or even a bicycle might fulfill that need at a lower cost.

A PROCESS FOR MINDFUL SPENDING

To think clearly about your expenses, start by asking these three questions for every purchase:

- What is the need?

- How often will I use this?

- Can I meet this need in a less expensive way?

Let's consider the example of Trevor, who we met in an earlier chapter. He's thinking about buying a truck. The first question he asks himself is "What need am I trying to meet?" If the answer is transportation, he then considers how often he'll actually use the truck. Will it be his main vehicle, or does his household already have other cars? Could buying a smaller car, taking public transit, or carpooling meet the same need at a lower cost?

What makes this decision trickier are the psychological benefits. Trevor might simply love trucks. Maybe owning one just makes him happy, even if he rarely uses the truck bed for hauling anything heavy. And that's valid. His money should support his happiness. But by identifying that the *need* is transportation, and that the *want* is the emotional satisfaction of owning a truck, Trevor can reframe the choice. Instead of defaulting to "I like trucks, so I'll buy one," he can evaluate the decision more clearly and decide whether the happiness it brings is worth the cost.

Let's see how Trevor might consider these questions.

- **What is the need?** *I need to replace my car, which I have to drive five days a week to work. I'd like to get something big enough that can safely transport my mountain bike when I want to go riding on the weekends.*

- **How often will I use this?** *Five days of driving to work and at least one day on the weekend for bike riding. I can also help out my friends who might need the truck bed and don't have their own trucks.*

- **Can I meet this need in a less expensive way?** *There's no public transportation where I live, so I definitely need a vehicle—and I will stick with buying used. I could buy a car instead and find one with a* *hitch so I can use a rack to hold my bike. This would also get better gas mileage, and insurance might be cheaper than on a truck.*

Let's look at another example: Maya is thinking about upgrading to the newest smartphone. She asks herself, "What need am I trying to meet?" If the answer is basic communication—calling, texting, using apps—then her current phone still does the job. So why is she drawn to the upgrade?

That's where the emotional layer comes in. Maya might love the excitement of new tech. Maybe she enjoys the sleek design, the better camera, or the feeling of staying current. And there's nothing wrong with that. But by recognizing that the *need* is basic communication and the *want* is the emotional satisfaction of owning the latest model, she can reframe the choice. Instead of thinking, "The latest phone is *so cool*, I want it!" and jumping to buy, Maya can step back and weigh whether those added emotional benefits are worth the cost—especially if other financial goals are on the horizon.

Let's see how Maya thinks through her decision to upgrade her phone:

- **What is the need?** *I need a phone that works reliably for texting, call-ing, and using apps like maps, banking, and social media. My current phone still does all of that without major issues, but it's just not as cool as a new phone!*

- **How often will I use this?** *I use my phone every day, pretty much all day—for work, communication, entertainment, and staying organized. But most of that use doesn't require the newest features.*

- **Can I meet this need in a less expensive way?** *Since my current phone still works well, I could hold off on upgrading until it starts to slow down or break. If I just want better pictures, I could invest in a high-end model from last year or buy refurbished to save money.*

There's no "correct" answer for either Trevor or Maya. What is optimal for them will depend on how much they decide they are willing to pay for the intangible benefits of the truck or phone.

By taking the time to reflect on these and other questions that might come to you, you can make spending decisions that align with your values and priorities, rather than acting on impulse or emotion. This process also helps you focus on what truly matters, avoiding wasteful purchases that add little to your happiness.

AN INTEGRATED METHOD

You may have noticed a considerable overlap among the last few chapters. The chapter on identifying needs talks about alternatives. The chapter on weighing costs against benefits talks about our needs. And, sure enough, this chapter on alternatives is discussing needs and costs.

This isn't because I am a bad writer or teacher (I hope!). It's because these questions are simply components of an integrated whole: a complete method for evaluating financial decisions.

This is what I meant in Chapter 1 when I said that these key questions are not steps in a process or discrete "levels" of analysis. They are deeply and irrevocably interconnected. You can't find effective alternatives to meet your needs if you haven't stopped to determine what needs you are trying to fulfill. You can't evaluate alternatives without adopting a cost/benefit method of evaluating each option. Each key question depends on the others, and each is needed for the foundation of the decision-making method which will help you execute your strategy and realize your vision for financial success.

I believe that it is this deep interconnection of multiple questions that makes it so difficult for financial teachers to convey how to think about money. It's just too much! Too much analysis, too many questions, too many alternatives. So they give up and settle on telling you rules to follow.

The three-question format presented here is my own personal method of breaking an intimidatingly complex approach to financial decision-making into manageable components. All you have to do is ask yourself the three questions one at a time, over and over, and you'll find yourself making better decisions. In time, this process of thinking will become much more natural and easier to implement.

PRACTICAL EXAMPLES

With that in mind, let's explore practical strategies for applying this method to your daily financial decisions. We will integrate our first two key questions into this process of identifying alternatives. By learning to distinguish between wants and needs and focusing on what truly matters, you can transform your financial habits and create a plan that supports the life you want to live.

Let's go back and expand on Trevor's desire to buy a truck. We already discussed his process in identifying his real need. Now he measures the costs and benefits of the options he identified. He does his research and finds that the model he wants would come with a $480 monthly loan payment. He's tempted to stop there. "I can afford $480 per month, so I'm going to buy it!" he thinks. Most people stop at this point and go buy the truck. Fortunately, Trevor digs a bit more and estimates that he will also spend $240 per month on gas, and $180 for insurance.

Trevor then decides to pause and reflect. His need is clear—he needs reliable transportation. He doesn't want to rely on the bus or a bike, so a personal vehicle is necessary. And he *can* afford the cost of the truck . . . but does he have to spend that much? Does it have to be a truck?

Could he find a cheaper alternative that would satisfy his needs first and his wants second?

After doing some comparison shopping, Trevor finds a used sedan that would meet his transportation needs just as well. The sedan would cost $340 per month on the loan, $180 for gas, and $100 for insurance. All in all, the truck would cost him $900 per month, while the sedan would cost $620—a difference of $280 per month.

By stepping back and evaluating, Trevor is finally in a position to ask the *real* question: "Is the added enjoyment of owning the truck worth $280 every month?"

That answer is completely up to him. But without asking all three key questions and employing our money method, Trevor wouldn't have had this moment of reflection. He probably would not have even recognized the trade-off. More importantly, he might not have realized how much of that $900 isn't paying for transportation—it's paying for the *feeling* of driving a truck. And the question "Do I want a truck?" is very different from "Do I want a truck *$280 more per month* than I want a sedan?"

Making that $280 per month tangible can be helpful in deciding if it is worthwhile: How many nights of takeout is that—two or three times per week at least? What could it turn into if he invested that in his retirement account? Could he use it to save up for a down payment on a house? How many weekend adventures or concert tickets could it buy?

Framing it this way helps Trevor make a decision that reflects what *really* matters to him when deciding if the truck is worth it or not. If he buys the truck, he does so knowing exactly what he is giving up to get it, and he's okay with it. If he passes on the truck and buys the sedan instead, then he can enjoy the sedan more knowing that his decision to buy it bought him $280 per month worth of other purchases. Either way, he is happier with his decision. Mission accomplished, Trevor!

THE CHOICE: EVALUATING ALTERNATIVES

In the last chapter, I talked about my desire to buy a lightsaber. You may have finished that section and concluded that I did not buy one. The truth is that I didn't buy one . . . I bought two! I bided my time, did some research, and watched. I watched for so long that I actually gave up and resigned myself to never owning a lightsaber. But then one day I spotted an ad on social media. Lightsabers on sale—two for $160! That price was much more consistent with how I expected to use a lightsaber. I caved to lifelong temptation and hit Buy.

These lightsabers aren't the prettiest. But they are strong and durable and tons of fun to swing around. My nieces and nephews can battle to their hearts' content, and I have no fear of the toys being damaged. For a reasonable cost, they get used regularly and have been a lot of fun. If I had not been patient and put my desires on hold while I did some research and watched for sales, I would have spent a lot of money on a delicate toy that could only be displayed. While I know many others buy a lightsaber for this exact purpose, I personally would have felt regret at that purchase.

Let me emphasize again that there is absolutely nothing wrong with spending money on things that bring you joy simply because they bring you joy. The goal is not to avoid spending, but rather to spend intentionally, knowing how much you are paying for which pleasures. Many purchases cost a significant amount but provide very little pleasure. By carefully considering alternatives, we can avoid those less fulfilling expenditures.

Let's consider a few additional scenarios to illustrate how evaluating alternatives can lead to better financial decisions:

What You're Buying	What You Think You Need	The Real Need	Alternatives
A restaurant meal	Tacos	Nutrition and time with friends	Cooking a delicious meal at home, hosting a potluck, or cooking together with friends
A trendy outfit	A "drip fit" to impress others	Protection and self-expression	Thrift stores, clothing swaps, or buying timeless, versatile pieces
A new video game	To reach level 100	Rest and entertainment	Free or low-cost options like borrowing or subscribing to games, enjoying nature, exploring hobbies
Meal delivery	A hot, ready-to-eat meal	Nutrition and convenience	Cooking quick meals at home or using meal prep services; prepping meals at home ahead of time

TABLE 5.1

WHY ALTERNATIVES MATTER

Exploring alternatives isn't about depriving yourself; it's about making informed decisions that maximize the value of your money. By identifying the true need behind a purchase, you can assess whether there are more cost-effective ways to achieve the same outcome. This process doesn't just save money—it also encourages creativity and mindfulness, helping you align your spending with your values and long-term goals.

For larger purchases, evaluating alternatives becomes even more critical. Buying a home is often driven by the need for shelter, but the way we meet that need can vary widely depending on our circumstances and priorities. Renting might be a better fit for some lifestyles and financial situations, providing flexibility and lower up-front costs. For those committed to owning their home, alternatives such as a smaller house, a fixer-upper, or a house in a different neighborhood could satisfy the need for shelter while significantly reducing costs.

Buying a car is often driven by the need for transportation, but how we choose to meet that need can vary significantly. For some, a used car, public transit, or a car pool might fulfill the need while reducing costs. For those who prefer driving newer vehicles, leasing could also be a viable option, without the long-term commitment of ownership. While a single car purchase may not seem overly impactful, the pattern of how, when, and why we buy cars throughout our lives can have an even greater financial impact than our housing decisions.

Additionally, the way you finance large purchases can dramatically affect how much they cost. For example, choosing a fifteen-year mortgage over a thirty-year mortgage typically results in lower interest paid over the life of the loan, although it requires higher monthly payments. These financing decisions can have a profound impact on the affordability and long-term financial implications of your purchase. We'll explore these financing strategies in greater detail in later chapters.

Even for smaller purchases, evaluating alternatives can make a big difference over time. For instance, consider groceries: Do you need to buy organic produce, or could conventionally grown fruits and vegetables meet your nutritional needs at a lower cost? When it comes to coffee, could making coffee at home provide the same satisfaction as a daily trip to the coffee shop? Similarly, for streaming services, ask yourself if you really need subscriptions to multiple platforms, or if one or two could meet your entertainment needs just as well.

PRACTICAL STEPS FOR EVALUATING ALTERNATIVES

1. **Identify the Real Need:** Start by asking yourself, "What am I really trying to achieve with this purchase?"

2. **Consider Less Expensive Options:** Brainstorm ways to meet your need that might cost less. Get creative and think outside the box. Discuss the issue with trusted friends and family, look online for ideas, or consult an AI to help you brainstorm alternatives. Be careful of taking advice from social media—people there may have motives other than your best interests at heart.

3. **Weigh the Trade-offs:** Evaluate whether the savings from an alternative are worth any potential sacrifices. For example, cooking at home saves money but takes time. Is the trade-off acceptable to you?

4. **Experiment and Reflect:** Try alternatives and reflect on the experience. Did the alternative meet your need? Did it provide the same level of satisfaction as the original option? If you took a less expensive alternative, how much money did you save, and what could you do with that money?

ALTERNATIVES AS SELF-DEFENSE

Evaluating alternatives is an incredibly powerful way to protect yourself from being manipulated by salesmen. It's important to remember that companies are not your friends. Their primary objective is to make money, and they achieve that only when you give them your money. Whether you're dealing with car dealerships, mortgage brokers, door-to-door salesmen, or even big box stores, their goal is to serve their interests—not yours. A core sales technique is to do everything possible to prevent you from exploring alternatives. By locking you into speaking or negotiating only with them, they gain power over the transaction and can maximize their profit at your expense.

Be skeptical and expect to have to fight for your own interests. For example, a store pushing an extended warranty on your new gaming console or TV isn't doing so out of concern for you; they're doing it because it's profitable for them. Their profit, after all, comes out of your pocket. Companies also use tactics like time limits ("Hurry in while supplies last" or "This deal is only good for ten minutes") to pressure you into rushing your purchase.

However, sales come back, prices change, and many "time-limited" offers are simply tricks to stop you from researching and considering alternatives. For instance, a website's five-minute countdown on a sale will likely reset every time you visit. Recognizing these tactics helps you stay in control of the transaction and make decisions on your terms. Be patient and take your time to find alternatives. It's worth it.

EMPOWERING YOUR FINANCIAL CHOICES

By learning to evaluate alternatives, you give yourself more control over your financial life. You're no longer limited to the default option or swayed by marketing and social pressures. Instead, you become an empowered decision-maker, capable of aligning your spending with your priorities and maximizing the value of every dollar. This process takes time and effort, but the potential savings are immense. In the short run, evaluating alternatives can save you hundreds of dollars on individual purchases. Over a lifetime, depending on the circumstances and nature of the decisions, it could add up to savings in the millions.

I can hear you scoffing through the page. Millions? Surely I am being dramatic.

Let's revisit our friend Trevor. If he decides to buy the truck, he is spending $280 per month more than is strictly necessary to meet his needs. Let's do some math on that $280 per month.

First, some assumptions. Let's assume Trevor is thirty years old and can earn 9 percent average in the stock market. Let's also assume that he replaces his truck every time the lease or the loan expires. That means he can invest $280 per month for thirty-five years until he is sixty-five. The result: $823,000 in his retirement account. If he is using a 401(k) plan that has a 50 percent match on contributions, that means his company will put in $140 to go with his $280, for a total of $420 per month. That would grow to $1.2 million. At 100 percent match, it grows to $1.6 million. This doesn't even factor in inflation. If the payments grow at even 2 percent per year to track with a 100 percent match *and* inflation, he'll have $2.4 million as he approaches retirement age.

Now, you can poke holes in these assumptions and change them around, but you can't get around the fact that even a small amount of monthly savings over time grows to a lot of money and security. Maybe you aren't deciding to buy a truck, or you do buy a truck but keep it for twenty years, so you think this math doesn't apply to you.

It does.

Maybe you're not buying a new truck every five years. But what if you could cut your spending by $280 per month just by being more efficient in a number of smaller decisions every month? Save $20 on groceries here, $10 on a tank of gas there, $30 on a pair of shoes, et cetera, until you had $280 over the course of the month to set aside for retirement? If you could do that, you could be the recipient of these tremendous benefits! You could have this math working for you every bit as much as Trevor could!

That's why I talk about this as a permanent mindset. It's not just for big decisions. It applies to smaller ones. Start asking these key questions and practice this process for as many decisions as you reasonably can. Doing so will gradually start to turn around your financial trajectory. I know it's work, and I know it's not easy. But by investing the time and effort up front, you can set the foundation for a more financially secure and fulfilling future.

MOMENTS OF CLARITY

This chapter explored the power of identifying your *real* needs and thoughtfully evaluating the *alternatives* available to meet them. Rather than defaulting to the easiest or flashiest option, remember to step back, ask the right questions, and reflect on whether the cost of a purchase truly matches the benefit it brings.

- **Distinguish wants from needs.** Needs are essential to well-being. Wants add enjoyment. Knowing the difference creates clarity—not judgment.

- **Embrace alternatives.** A cheaper or simpler option may meet your need just as well, freeing up money for things that matter more.

- **This is a lifelong tool, not a one-time trick.** Evaluating alternatives works for both big and small decisions. Build the habit now and it will serve you for life.

- **Big costs come from patterns, not just purchases.** Watch your patterns of spending. Individual purchases may not be that impactful by themselves, but a pattern of spending more and getting less has a huge impact on your long-term financial well-being.

CHAPTER SIX

YOUR MONEY PERSONALITY

They say the man who invented the roller coaster was a genius. A true visionary. He dreamed in loops and hills, in speed and screams of joy. He didn't want to build just another ride—he wanted to create an *experience*. And when he finally finished designing his masterpiece—an elegant tangle of wooden tracks and dizzying drops—he stood back, proud and exhilarated.

His colleague, Ed, was a different kind of thinker. Less flash, more function. While the inventor dreamed of thrills, Ed thought about safety. Structure. How to stop without derailing.

"Hey," Ed said, peering over the plans, "how do you plan to stop this thing?"

The inventor blinked. "Huh. Hadn't thought of that."

Oops.

He was so focused on what the ride *could do*—how fast it could go, how thrilling it could be—that he didn't stop to think about how it would *end*.

And that's how Ed, the unsung hero of roller coaster history, invented the roller coaster brake.

Now here's the thing—neither of them could have done it alone. Without the thrill-seeker, there would be no roller coaster. Without Ed the brake guy, there'd be no riders coming back in one piece. Together, they made something remarkable.

ALL TYPES OF MONEY MINDS

Okay, you got me. This roller coaster story is completely made up.

I share it only because it reminds me of how different personality types approach life and money. Some people are risk takers. They think big, move fast, chase opportunities, and see potential everywhere. Others are the steady hands—the planners, the question-askers, the ones who make sure there's a safety net before anyone takes a leap. Some of us are building the track; others are engineering the brakes. But all of us are needed.

We don't all have to approach life the same way. In fact, it's better when we don't. What matters is learning to value what each person brings to the table. The ride works best when we design it together.

I've spent a lot of time in this book so far talking about the need to deeply and accurately understand your thoughts, feelings, values, and priorities. That's a harder task than it might seem on the surface. To help you out, I've provided an assessment to help you evaluate and understand your own emotional attitudes towards money. This collection of feelings and attitudes is known as your money personality.

Begin by taking the money personality assessment below to help you identify your money personality. Do this before reading about the personality types so you don't accidentally steer your answers towards the personality you wish you had. Full self-honesty is essential, and lying to yourself to make yourself feel better is only going to hurt you more. Just keep in mind that there is no such thing as a better or worse money personality. They all have advantages and they all have weaknesses.

THE MONEY PERSONALITY ASSESSMENT

To complete this assessment and get an evaluation of your money personality, simply answer each of the following questions as honestly as possible. Then, use the scoring sheet to count how many answers you selected for each personality.

1. Where does most of your money typically end up?
   a. Covering bills, debt payments, or daily expenses
   b. Sitting safely in my bank account
   c. Locked into real estate or stock investments
   d. Going toward major purchases like home upgrades or a new vehicle

2. What would you do if $1,000,000 landed in your lap today?
   a. Host an unforgettable celebration for everyone I care about
   b. Park it in savings and call my financial planner immediately
   c. Launch a passion project or business I've been planning
   d. Upgrade my living space and ride

3. How would you sum up your attitude toward money?
   a. It's limited—spend with caution
   b. Life is short, enjoy what money can buy while you can
   c. Money helps create a meaningful lifestyle for me and my loved ones
   d. Money is unpredictable, so enjoy it when you have it

4.   What's your favorite way to use your downtime?

   a.   Going on trips or shopping adventures

   b.   Free or low-cost activities that bring joy

   c.   Enhancing my home, car, wardrobe, or other possessions

   d.   Brainstorming and building new ideas or side hustles

5.   Which of these concerns hits closest to home?

   a.   I make decent income but can't seem to build savings

   b.   I save regularly, but the growth is slow

   c.   My financial risks sometimes create stress in my relationships

   d.   I often spend more than planned—it's hard to resist

6.   What do others tend to think about your financial habits?

   a.   I'm generous and often share freely

   b.   I'm cautious and budget-conscious

   c.   I look affluent because of how I live

   d.   I'm skilled at making smart investment moves

7.   When you make purchases, what describes you best?

   a.   I follow my heart and buy what brings joy, even spontaneously

   b.   I dig into reviews and price comparisons first

   c.   I limit spending to essentials and prefer to invest the rest

   d.   I value durable, high-quality items—even if they're pricey

8.   How do you approach retirement saving?

   a.   I contribute to retirement steadily from each paycheck

   b.   I plan to save more once I've handled other financial priorities

   c.   I'm building wealth through assets I plan to sell later

   d.   I haven't made retirement savings a focus

9. How do you handle day-to-day money management?

    a. I sometimes lose control or overspend

    b. I track every dollar and stick to a budget

    c. I earn well but often wonder where the money goes

    d. I take bold steps with money and usually come out ahead

10. A trusted friend offers you a chance to invest $25,000 in their new venture. You respond . . .

    a. Yes—even if it means borrowing some of the funds

    b. Yes, but only if I have the cash available

    c. No, I'm not comfortable with the risk

    d. No, I'd rather enjoy spending that money personally

11. What's your approach to buying a home?

    a. It feels out of reach—I'd love one but doubt I can afford my ideal

    b. I'd choose something well within my financial comfort zone

    c. I'd go for the dream home, even if it means some lifestyle cuts

    d. I'd buy modestly for myself to invest in additional properties

12. How do you use credit cards?

    a. I avoid them entirely

    b. Several of my cards are at or near their limits

    c. I use available credit responsibly and pay down balances monthly

    d. I'd use a card to fund a promising investment if needed

SCORING

Use the table below to identify the personality code that corresponds to your answer for each question. For example, if you selected A for question 1, then write a P next to question 1. If you answered B for question 2, put an S next to question 2. If you answered D to question 3, put an E as the code for question 3. Continue until you have identified the code for each question. Then add up how many of each code you have. The code that you have the most of is your dominant money personality.

	Answer			
	A	B	C	D
Question 1	P	S	E	R
Question 2	P	S	E	R
Question 3	S	P	R	E
Question 4	P	S	R	E
Question 5	R	S	E	P
Question 6	P	S	R	E
Question 7	P	S	E	R
Question 8	S	R	E	P
Question 9	P	S	R	E
Question 10	E	R	S	P
Question 11	P	S	R	E
Question 12	S	P	R	E

FIGURE 6.1. Scoring Card

It is common for people to have tendencies in several different money personalities. The point of this exercise is not to try to lock your personality into a little box, but to help you increase your awareness of your relative strengths and weaknesses so you can plan accordingly.

Before we discuss what the letters P, R, E, and S mean in your personality score, let's first talk about three important factors that influenced your answers, as these will be important to know when we discuss your type, including how to make improvements. These three factors are: motivation, time orientation, and risk tolerance.

MOTIVATION

What makes you want to spend money? What emotional response do you have toward various kinds of spending? These internal characteristics influence your money behavior and determine what you value the most. Understanding your motivations is important because they determine how much utility you will get from a purchase. If you buy something that doesn't appeal to your motivations, you won't be likely to enjoy it very much.

It is common for our motivations to be subconscious. This means that you might be affected by them without you even knowing it. This is why it is important to regularly stop yourself when you are about to make a purchase. Just pause and think about why you want to spend your money on this particular item. Is it because it really will bring you utility? Or is it more of an instinctive motivation? After you make a purchase, pause and ask yourself, "How do I feel as a result of this purchase?" These emotional reactions speak to your motivations and give you a better sense of how you can manage your emotional state, rather than letting your emotions control you and your spending.

TIME ORIENTATION

Do you think more about the present or the future? The second aspect of your money personality is your time orientation. Some people are future oriented. This means that they are willing to sacrifice their present well-being for their future well-being. Future-oriented people are willing to make today worse so their tomorrow can be better. People who are extremely future-oriented can even be excited to sacrifice for the future. Future-oriented people tend to be natural savers. They prefer to save for tomorrow even if it means having less today.

Other people are present-oriented. This means that they value their present well-being more than their future well-being. People who are present-oriented don't tend to worry about the future. They prefer to live in the moment. They stop and smell the roses. They don't let the worry of what *could* happen ruin what is actually happening now. Present-oriented people tend to know instinctively how to use their money to make life better now.

RISK TOLERANCE

How comfortable are you with uncertainty? The third aspect of your money personality is your risk tolerance. Some people are tolerant of risk. The uncertainty of the unknown does not frighten them. They can take risks and leap into the unknown with relatively little concern. Some people can be so risk tolerant that they even come to enjoy the uncertainty of risk. Risk-tolerant people tend to make good use of the stock market. They do not let the fear of possibly losing money stop them from taking advantage of investing in the stock market.

Others are risk averse. The presence of uncertainty makes their emotions squirm. The fear of losing something they treasure can sometimes be paralyzing. People who are highly risk averse sometimes avoid investing in the stock market. However, when they do, they tend to do very well because they don't take too much risk. Taking too much risk with investments is the number one reason why people sometimes get bad results from the stock market. Risk-averse individuals rarely lose money in the stock market because they don't take too much risk.

We use these criteria to categorize money personalities into four broad types which correlate to the P, R, E, and S scores from your money personality quiz: *Pleasure, Recognition, Entrepreneurial,* and *Security.* Each personality type is labeled by their top priority—pleasure types prioritize pleasure and fun, while entrepreneurs focus on making money. Recognition types prize being seen to be successful (however they define success), and security types prioritize safety.

It's essential to note that humans are complex beings. No human can be reduced down into just one of four categories. Everyone has at least some tendency towards each type of money personality. However, each person also usually has one money personality that describes them better than the others. This dominant money personality is what we call your money personality.

You can think of your money personality as your gut instinct. Some people's instincts tell them to avoid risk, while other people's instincts tell them to take risks. Some people prefer to save their money for a rainy day, while others prefer to live in the moment and spend their money now.

There is no right or wrong money personality. The world needs people of all personality types to function properly. Being aware of the nature of your own money personality will help you to be able to identify when it might be about to lead you into a mistake. For example, those who have the security personality might purchase too much insurance, while people who are more entrepreneurial might be vulnerable to take too much risk with their investments.

THE PERSONALITIES

Now it's time to revisit the P-R-E-S scores in that money personality quiz and see what kind of a spender you are. To score your quiz, simply add up how many of each letter you answered. The more of each letter you have, the more dominant that personality type is for you. The personality with the highest score is your dominant money personality.

You will almost certainly have some of each personality type in your scores. That's good and normal. Focus in on the top one or two to get the best sense of your overall money personality. But don't let this focus on your money personality drive your choices. Like with astrology, people are sometimes prone to saying, "I can't do that because I'm a security personality." The reality is that you are so much more than this simple personality type. This is just a little exercise to give you a chance to consider your responses to these quiz questions. As with everything, you will need to adapt this information to your use.

As an example, my score on the quiz looks like this—

- P = 0
- R = 5
- E = 1
- S = 6

According to my quiz results, my dominant money personality is security, but I have a strong bent towards recognition. That makes sense to me, since security has always been the number one priority for me financially, but when I do spend I am willing to spend for quality goods that provide lasting function and value.

PLEASURE PERSONALITY

The pleasure money personality is characterized by people who are risk tolerant and present-oriented. They take risks with their money and with their experiences for the sheer enjoyment of it. These people enjoy having fun and experiencing new adventures more than they enjoy accumulating wealth. The pleasure personalities tend to pursue high-income careers because they often enjoy expensive lifestyles. They also often enjoy the immediacy of shopping. Those with this personality are the most likely to enjoy retail therapy—buying things to make oneself feel better. This tendency to shop for fun or relaxation can lead them to carry high credit card balances.

These people are often the ones who make the world fun! They invent skydiving, roller coasters, and amusement parks. These are pleasures that many people enjoy, even if they are not pleasure personality types themselves.

Those with the pleasure personality need to be cautious. They often struggle to control their spending. Their desire for immediate excitement can lead them to become compulsive gamblers. They may need to employ external commitment devices to help them control their spending behavior and save for the future.

RECOGNITION PERSONALITY

The recognition money personality is risk averse and present-oriented. Recognition personality people prefer not to take large risks. They have a strong desire to succeed and excel. They often display their wealth through the living of expensive lifestyles. Like the pleasure personality, these people tend to be ambitious in their careers and education.

The motivation behind this ambition is very different for recognition personalities. Those with this dominant personality prefer to spend their money on the best goods and services. They frequently purchase designer clothes, private educations, and luxurious homes and cars.

Recognition personalities are present-oriented like the pleasure personality, but instead of purchasing experiences, they purchase items of lasting value. People like this are great because they like to make the world beautiful. These are the people who design luxurious resorts, hotels, cars, and clothes. Yet this personality type does have its own problems. They need to be careful not to get too carried away with their spending and their lifestyle. Those who go too far in this personality become poseurs and are perceived as being fake or inauthentic. Those with this money personality need to be careful of their spending.

ENTREPRENEUR PERSONALITY

Those with the entrepreneurial motivation take large risks with their money, not for pleasure but in the hope of increasing their wealth. They are often the people who produce the most wealth in the world. These people are very future oriented. They would rather sacrifice and work today so that they can be wealthy tomorrow. The entrepreneurial types often succeed without formal education or high income. They frequently use someone else's wealth to create wealth of their own. To this personality type, money represents an opportunity to realize their passion for generating wealth.

These people benefit the world by making it progressive and wealthy. These are the people who invent the airplanes and assembly lines that move the rest of the world forward. When taken to extremes, people of this personality type run the risk of becoming swindlers: people who will do anything to make money. The greatest challenge faced by the entrepreneur personality is that they tend to take on too much risk. They can be a millionaire one day and completely bankrupt the next!

SECURITY PERSONALITY

Those with the security money personality place a high priority on safety. They tend to avoid risk and place a strong emphasis on securing their future. These people manage and save their money naturally and instinctively. They prefer to have a budget and know exactly where their money is going. Security personalities invest conservatively. They prefer to earn less interest in favor of decreasing their investment risk. They tend to feel uncomfortable with debt and therefore carry little or none of it. They are often wary of using credit cards at all.

These people keep the world safe. These are the people who invent airbags and antilock brakes. But if the security personality becomes too strong, this type of person can become a chronic hoarder. They can get stuck in the saving mentality and forget to actually use their money to make their lives better. They face being too conservative in their investments and missing out on good opportunities to grow their wealth.

MAKING THE MOST OF YOUR OWN PERSONALITY

Now that you've discovered which money personality best fits you, the next question is naturally, *What can you do with that insight?* Understanding your financial tendencies isn't just interesting, it's powerful. When you know how you're wired to think about money, you can start designing strategies that play to your strengths and protect against your blind spots. This awareness is the first step toward making smarter, more sustainable financial decisions that actually work for you.

Remember Trevor? He had his eye on a brand-new truck—the kind that practically announces success when it rolls up. But when he took a step back and thought about his bigger goals, he realized that what mattered more was saving for the home he wanted.

Trevor took the test and realized he had a recognition money personality. He's driven by the desire to succeed and be seen as successful. That insight helped him recognize *why* the truck mattered to him—it wasn't just transportation, it was a symbol. He liked that people were impressed with this truck. Without having taken the money personality test, he might not have known that his desire for recognition was part of the need the truck would fulfill, and he might have ended up dissatisfied with his truck.

This dissatisfaction would have been a problem because it would have itched under his skin and annoyed him every day. Eventually, he likely would have caved and traded in his truck. Or he would have taken a doubly bad path and wound up buying *two* trucks; not realizing that for him, his desire for recognition was an integral part of the value of the truck.

Once he understood his money personality, he found a smarter path: He bought a reliable used truck and spent a little extra on a sleek paint job. The result? A head-turning truck for considerably less than the cost of a new truck.

Knowing his personality also helped Trevor realize he needed to set up a spending safeguard: a forty-eight-hour waiting rule for any purchase over $300. As someone less tempted by impulse buys and more likely to overspend on big-ticket items, this rule helped him pause and evaluate whether a purchase truly aligned with his goals.

Trevor didn't give up recognition, he just found a way to enjoy it without letting it drive his finances off course.

My former student Jenna, as you might remember, wasn't spending thousands at a time, but the purchases added up: a new pair of sandals here, a cute tumbler there; the kind of shopping that felt like self-care in the moment.

Jenna has a pleasure money personality. She's present-focused and drawn to experiences, comfort, and the emotional lift that comes from something new. Knowing that about herself changed everything.

She realized her temptation wasn't big splurges but small, frequent pick-me-ups. So she set a lower spending threshold than Trevor—just $50—for her pause-and-think rule. Anything over that, she had to wait twenty-four hours. She also gave herself a clever boundary: no more than twenty-five pairs of shoes. If she wants a new pair, one has to go. That really made it easier for her to realize when the new shoes were going to "upgrade" her lifestyle, and when they were just going to sit and collect dust.

Jenna didn't cut out fun from her life—she made room for it. She reduced spending on her car and other "boring" stuff so she could say yes more often to concerts, weekend getaways, and dinners with friends. Critically, she made her savings automatically deposit, so the fun money was just that—*leftover*, not borrowed from her future. Instead of trying to change her personality, Jenna learned to work with it. She still finds joy in the moment, but now it's joy she can actually afford and which doesn't compromise her security, her future, or her larger goals.

Then there's Diego. While his friends were climbing corporate ladders, Diego was sketching business plans on napkins and flipping sneakers for profit in high school. He's always had the entrepreneur money personality—future-focused, risk-tolerant, and obsessed with turning ideas into income.

For Diego, money is fuel. He doesn't chase status or comfort—he chases opportunity. That drive helped him launch a side hustle that turned into a full-time gig before he even graduated high school. But it also led him into trouble. One month he'd land a big client; the next he'd barely cover rent, after dumping his savings into a new marketing campaign that flopped.

The problem wasn't ambition, it was instability. So Diego got strategic. He now splits every paycheck: 70 percent for business and life, 30 percent into a "resilience fund" to cover at least six months of lean time. And he made another new rule: He has to walk through any investment over $1,000 with a mentor. If he can't clearly define the worst-case scenario, he doesn't pull the trigger.

Diego didn't tone down his entrepreneurial spirit. He just gave it a safety net and a filter. Now, he's still all-in on the future, but with smarter plays, steadier ground, and fewer crash landings.

Me? I've got a blend of security and recognition in my money personality today. But back in the day I was all security, all the time. I lived in constant fear of running out of money. Every dollar had a job, and none of those jobs was fun.

To be fair, that mindset served me well. While most of my peers were just getting started financially, I had stability. But it came at a cost: I missed out on a lot of joy. I was safe, but not happy.

Over the last decade I've worked to retrain that part of myself. One of my proudest moments of financial growth wasn't a big investment win—it was buying those lightsabers. Not because I needed them, but because I wanted them. It was therapy. A test. Could I let myself buy something *just* because I wanted it?

And guess what? The world didn't fall apart. I didn't go broke. I just had fun and let my inner child finally have something he'd wanted for a very long time.

The tools I use are a little different from the others I've described. I created a joy fund—a monthly chunk of money I can spend guilt-free. I also made a rule that for every dollar I put in my emergency fund or save for retirement, I allow myself a small slice to put into the joy fund so I don't forget to enjoy the journey. I've learned that you can have fun and still be careful. I didn't stop protecting my future; I just finally let my money support the present, too.

MONEY PERSONALITIES: A FINAL REFLECTION

You've just read four very different stories from four people with distinct money personalities. But here's the truth: *No one is just one type.* We all carry pieces of each personality inside us. The goal isn't to label yourself and stay stuck there. It's to gain insight into the unique way that you think and feel about money, and how that shapes your behavior.

That insight starts with introspection. When you understand your money personality, you start to see the patterns behind your gut instincts. And while your gut can be a powerful guide, it can also mislead you. Trevor's instinct told him a truck that turned heads would make him feel successful. Jenna's told her that cute shoes would bring happiness. Mine told me that if I spent $5 on fast food I would run out of money. None of these is entirely wrong, but none convey the full story either.

Knowing your personality helps you recognize those instincts for what they are: *signals*, not commands. You don't need to kill those feelings. In fact, trying to suppress them can backfire. You're not broken—you're unique. And your emotional reactions to money can become powerful tools if you learn to harness them.

FEELINGS AND INSTINCTS ARE SIGNALS, NOT COMMANDS.

Tie your biggest goals *to* your instincts. If you lean towards pleasure, build fun rewards into your savings journey.

My wife loved when we moved our car loan from the bank that held it to the credit union we use for our daily banking. She loved this because she could see the loan balance every week, and it motivated her to attack the balance and pay it off. The visible reminder she got when she went to pay bills motivated her powerfully in ways that neither of us had anticipated. If you're entrepreneurial, give yourself permission to expand your business *after* securing the boring-but-essential insurance. If you crave recognition, find ways to have nice things that don't wreck your budget. And if you're security focused like I once was, practice letting a little joy into your spreadsheets.

You don't need to change your personality. You just need to understand it and then build a system that works *with* it instead of against it. While this is not an easy task, it is something that the strategy approach can help you accomplish. That's what this whole book is about: not just building a financial plan but creating a strategy that equips you to make thoughtful decisions. This is done by routinely asking the three key questions:

1. What's the purpose of the purchase?
2. Is it worth the cost?
3. Is there a smart swap?

What I love about this strategic approach is that it goes deeper than dollars and cents. It gives you structure for your finances and insight into your motivations. It connects your daily decisions to your deeper vision. It turns your gut reactions into learning opportunities instead of liabilities.

Your vision should reflect what you truly want out of life, and that vision should align with your money personality, because your personality shapes what brings you the most joy and meaning. When you consistently apply this strategy—asking the three questions, reflecting on your choices, staying focused on your vision and goals—you're not just managing money. You're discovering who you are, how you operate, and how to make your financial life serve *you*.

MOMENTS OF CLARITY

- **Awareness is your superpower.** Understanding your personality helps you identify the emotional triggers behind your financial decisions, which gives you the ability to plan smarter and avoid regret.

- **No one is just one type.** You're likely a mix of all the P-R-E-S types: Pleasure, Recognition, Entrepreneurial, and Security. The key is to identify which ones drive your behavior the most, and where they may lead you astray.

- **Your instincts aren't commands.** Whether you crave fun, security, recognition, or opportunity, those instincts are signals to be interpreted, not orders to obey. Learning to pause, reflect, and redirect can make all the difference.

- **Build systems that align with your style.** From pause rules to joy funds to mentor checklists, creating personal rules that match your tendencies will help you succeed without having to fight your natural instincts.

- **Use your personality to fuel your vision.** Instead of trying to force yourself into a one-size-fits-all budget, shape your financial strategy around what brings you meaning, joy, and motivation.

- **Strategy beats willpower.** You don't need more discipline— you need a system that works *with* your personality and vision. That's why this book emphasizes a strategy-based approach over rigid plans.

PART 2

EMPOWERED SPENDING

CHAPTER SEVEN

YOUR MONEY AND YOUR MIND

I have a confession: I hate exercise. I don't mean I'd "rather not" exercise—I mean my brain throws a full-blown tantrum every time I try. The moment I lace up my sneakers and press play on the workout video, it starts pounding on the inside of my skull like a protest drummer at a City Hall rally: *Stop! Stop! Stop!*

And yet I don't hate physical work. I'll haul bricks across the yard, build a shed, rip out drywall, and climb up and down a ladder all afternoon without a complaint. In fact, I often enjoy the physical exertion of working on a home project. But the second my brain registers that I'm lifting this weight for the sole purpose of "exercise," it stages a rebellion.

Maybe this is how most people feel about studying. I've always loved to study, loved the clarity of a well-organized outline or the satisfaction of mastering a concept. But I've heard enough groans from students to know that for many, studying feels like punishment. That's what exercise is for me: academic torture for the body.

But I wanted to change, be healthier, have more energy, all that great stuff that exercise is supposed to bring. I told myself, "You just need a plan." So I made one. I set an alarm. Got the clothes. I even had my wife hold me accountable and taped a photo of myself with a digitally enhanced six-pack on the fridge (to her chagrin). I had a strategy. I built a plan to execute that strategy. I did everything right . . . except the part where I actually, you know, *exercised*.

The plan never made it off the page. And that's the trap we all fall into: the belief that having a strategy is the same as making progress. But a strategy without execution? That's just a really well-decorated to-do list.

In like manner, sitting down to dream up a vision; design a strategy; and set up a spending plan that reflects our highest wants and needs is fruitless if we can't get ourselves to follow through. And let's be honest—*this* is the hardest part. Not the dreaming. Not the planning. The execution. Actually doing the thing, day in and day out, when the novelty has worn off and your brain starts complaining. That's where the real work—and the real transformation—happens.

THE PROBLEM WITH DISCIPLINE

A lot of people believe their financial struggles come down to a lack of discipline. *If I just had more self-control, I wouldn't have these problems.* That's a half-truth—and like most half-truths, it can do more harm than good.

Yes, discipline is a valuable trait. But here's the problem: You can't just brute-force discipline into your brain. You can't snap your fingers and suddenly become someone who always makes perfect choices. And when people believe that's what they're supposed to do, it leaves them feeling broken, thinking, *I'm just not disciplined enough.* That kind of thinking doesn't motivate change—it reinforces shame. It makes us believe we're the problem, that we'll never be good with money, and that we might as well give up.

But it's not the end of the story.

We all have weak spots. I've got plenty of discipline when it comes to studying, budgeting, and writing. But exercise? That's a different story. And don't get me started on trying to reseal a bag of Cheetos. Once I start, I just might finish the whole bag, even though it makes me sick. We all have areas where self-control feels easy and other areas where it feels impossible. The mistake is comparing your weaknesses to someone else's strengths, then concluding you're just not cut out for success.

The truth is, our brains weren't built for personal finance. They didn't evolve to plan for retirement or juggle spending across decades. They evolved to help us hunt, gather, and run from things with teeth. Modern financial life moves a lot faster—and asks a lot more of us—than the brains we're working with were originally designed for.

It's no wonder so many of us struggle to keep up. It's not a flaw in your character to struggle with controlling spending impulses. It's just part of being human. Here's the good news: Once you understand how the human brain works in general—and how *your* brain works in particular—you can start designing better strategies. You can change the way you approach decisions in a way that works *with* your instincts, not against them. And that shift can dramatically improve your ability to follow through, stick to your plan, and actually reach your financial goals.

Let's look at a few ways our inner caveman still shows up in our money habits today:

- **We crave instant rewards.** Your ancestors didn't wait six months for a berry bush to grow—they ate what they found right away. That instinct hasn't gone away. It's why a flash sale or a surprise delivery on your doorstep feels so good—and why saving for a future vacation or retirement can feel . . . kind of boring.

- **We fear loss more than we value gain.** Back on the Savannah, losing your food or shelter could mean death. So today we still react emotionally when we see our investments drop or feel like we're missing out.

- **We're wired to follow the herd.** If the group ran, you ran. Peer pressure wasn't just social, it was a matter of survival. Today, that same instinct can push us to keep up with friends' spending habits, jump on financial fads, or chase trends we don't really understand just because everyone else is doing it.

- **We struggle with abstract, future-focused thinking.** Planning for something thirty years from now? We can do it, but that's not the primary function our brains evolved for. The long-term benefits of saving for retirement are intellectually clear but emotionally distant. That's why it's so hard to stay motivated when the payoff feels forever away.

Each of these tendencies represents a keen wisdom—if you're living in a cave and worried about saber-tooth tigers. But in modern life, those instincts can sabotage our best-laid financial plans. The goal isn't to erase these instincts. It's to understand them well enough to design systems that help us choose better, even when our wiring wants us to do otherwise.

LOOKING INSIDE

So why do we think this way—and more importantly, what can we do about it? To answer that, let's take a closer look at the physical structure of the brain and what each part actually does. Now, the brain is the most complex object humans have ever studied, so any explanation in a book like this will necessarily be a huge oversimplification. Still, it helps to know the basics.

Neuroeconomists often describe the human brain as essentially a mammalian brain with an upgraded cortex. In other words, it's built in layers—instinctive, emotional systems underneath, and more thoughtful, rational processing on top. As one neuroeconomist put it, "Human behavior will generally be a compromise between animal emotions and instincts, and human deliberation and foresight."[8]

That emotional, reactive part of the brain that I earlier called System 1 is the same part that drives snap spending and gut-level decisions. The more thoughtful, deliberate part of your brain lives in the prefrontal cortex, also known as System 2. Both systems have value and are essential to being human. But understanding how they interact—and sometimes conflict—is key to making better decisions.

One of my favorite ways to explain this idea comes from social psychologist Dr. Jonathan Haidt.[9] He offers a powerful visual: imagine your brain as a rider on the back of an elephant. The rider represents System 2—your logical, deliberate mind—while the elephant stands in for System 1—your fast, emotional, instinctive responses. It's a simple image, but it captures something deeply true about human behavior. The rider might hold the reins, but let's be honest: When the elephant wants to go somewhere, the rider's just along for the ride, unless there's a clear path and a good reason to steer otherwise.

The image of the rider and the elephant isn't just memorable. It's accurate in a way that most people feel in their daily lives, even if they've never put words to it. The rider, our System 2, is thoughtful, reflective, and goal-oriented. But compared to the elephant, System 2

---

8   Colin F. Camerer, George Loewenstein, and Drazen Prelec, "Neuroeconomics: Why Economics Needs Brains," *The Scandinavian Journal of Economics* 106, no. 3 (2004): 555–579.

9   Jonathan Haidt, "Moral Psychology and the Law: How Intuitions Drive Reasoning, Judgment, and the Search for Evidence," *Alabama Law Review* 64, no. 4 (2013): 867–880.

is small, slow, and easily exhausted. The elephant, on the other hand, is massive and powerful. It's driven by emotion, instinct, and habit. It reacts in milliseconds, often before the rider even realizes something happened.

This isn't a battle between equals. Not remotely. A person failing to stop a rampaging elephant isn't a failure—they are just much smaller than the elephant. The key, then, isn't to try to beat your worst impulses with sheet brute disciplinary power. It's to prevent, as much as possible, those impulses (the elephant) from taking control at all. To keep the analogy, the goal isn't to stop the elephant mid-rampage, it's to control the environment so that the elephant never gets upset enough to rampage in the first place.

You're probably familiar with this inner tug-of-war. You feel it every time you stand in front of the fridge debating whether to cook or give in to takeout again. Part of you is ready to spend $50 on dinner without blinking, and another part is whispering, "We could make something at home for five bucks and put the rest in savings." You feel it when you eye those new shoes. Part of you says, "Treat yourself," and the other part says, "I really shouldn't . . ."

It's not just about money, either. It shows up when you want to scroll on your phone but also want to read more. When you plan to wake up early but snooze the alarm. When you say yes to dessert and then remember you're trying to be healthier. That's the elephant and the rider in action. You're not broken—we're all just built that way. The real question isn't how to silence one voice or the other. It's how to get them working together.

The biggest mistake people make when battling their inner elephant is that they think they need to kill the elephant to succeed. They see the elephant as the enemy, and enemies are to be defeated, right? So they tell themselves: *Just be more rational. Squash your feelings and be more logical. More responsible. More disciplined. Power through temptation and just make good choices. Easy as pie.*

Except it's not, is it?

The elephant isn't trying to sabotage you. It's doing exactly what it evolved to do: stay alive, respond quickly to threats, seek rewards, and avoid discomfort. And for most of human history, that was incredibly useful. You didn't need to think through a step-by-step budget when your biggest financial decision was whether to trade three berries for a hunk of meat. But today, when every app is engineered to hijack attention, and every purchase is a tap away? That elephant gets led straight into financial traps.

What makes the metaphor even more apt is that while the rider has the ability to see further, plan ahead, and reason through consequences, it only works when the elephant is calm and the terrain is manageable. When you're stressed, tired, anxious, or even just hungry, the rider starts to lose control. And once the elephant starts charging—toward a shopping spree, a too-good-to-be-true investment, a new pair of shoes, or a fancy lightsaber—it's incredibly hard to stop.

So no, the answer isn't to become more like the rider and less like the elephant. It's to recognize that both are part of you. You don't win by wrestling the elephant—you win by learning how to guide it.

That's what a good financial strategy does. It builds paths the elephant naturally wants to follow. It sets up cues, defaults, and routines that make smart choices feel easy, because the elephant thinks they're the obvious direction to go.

HOW TO TRAIN YOUR ELEPHANT

Harnessing your elephant's power starts with understanding yourself. You can't guide what you don't understand. That's why the money personality assessment we covered earlier can be such a valuable tool: It offers insight into what your elephant wants. And once you know that, you can work *with* it instead of constantly fighting against it.

Take someone with a pleasure personality. Their elephant is wired to seek enjoyment in the moment. So instead of trying to force it to behave through sheer willpower, a smarter move is to use what already motivates it. A small, immediate reward like a coffee, a treat, or a guilt-free hour of screen time can be just enough to keep the elephant moving toward a bigger, long-term goal like saving for a trip or sticking to a budget. It's not bribery. It's smart behavioral design.

But that same approach might completely backfire for someone with a security personality—like me. My elephant doesn't find small spending rewarding. It finds it stressful. If you tell my elephant, "Buy yourself a treat to celebrate saving money," it'll tense up. It might even back away from saving altogether just to avoid having to spend on a reward. That's the thing: What motivates one elephant could totally derail another.

So the key isn't just building a financial system—it's building *your* financial system. One that's shaped around what energizes and calms your elephant, not someone else's. When you do that, financial discipline stops feeling like a battle and starts feeling like momentum.

Let's look at one of my favorite studies that illustrates this principle. In this study, participants were split into two groups. One group was asked to choose a snack to receive immediately, and 70 percent picked the tastier, unhealthy option. The second group chose a snack to be delivered in one week, with completely opposite results: only 26 percent of this group picked the unhealthy treat while 74 percent opted for the healthier choice. The conclusion is clear: The elephant wants the indulgence now, while the rider aspires to health in the future.

And when the two are in conflict in the present moment, the elephant almost always wins.[10]

That's the fundamental tension: We all have a system in our brain that can imagine the future . . . but it's riding on top of a system that doesn't care about the future at all. Understanding this is essential to building better habits. The elephant isn't going away—but you *can* train it, guide it, and even build a path it wants to walk.

MOMENTS OF CLARITY

- **Your brain wasn't built for modern finance.** It evolved for survival, not for long-term budgeting, retirement planning, or resisting online shopping carts.

- **Discipline isn't a switch you can flip.** Many people blame their struggles on a lack of willpower, but trying to brute-force discipline rarely works, and often leads to shame rather than change.

- **System 1 (the elephant) and System 2 (the rider) work together—but unequally.** The elephant is emotional, impulsive, and powerful. The rider is rational but limited in energy. When they disagree in the moment, the elephant usually wins.

- **Your money personality.** It reveals what your elephant craves, fears, and struggles with, giving you insight into how to motivate it effectively and avoid triggers that lead to poor decisions.

---

10 Daniel Read and Barbara van Leeuwen, "Predicting Hunger: The Effects of Appetite and Delay on Choice," *Organizational Behavior and Human Decision Processes* 76, no. 2 (1998): 189–205.

CHAPTER EIGHT

OUTSMARTING IMPULSE

I was meeting with a student recently, and after a long pause, she let out a sigh and said, "It just feels like money is my enemy— always one step ahead of me, always slipping through my fingers." She looked tired. Frustrated. Like she'd been fighting a losing battle she didn't fully understand.

She went on to describe how no matter how carefully she tried to plan, something always seemed to come up: a birthday dinner, a last-minute textbook, a sale too good to pass up. "It's like I try to do everything right," she said, "but my money still disappears. I don't even know where it goes half the time." Her words weren't just about numbers. They were about defeat. Shame. Feeling like she wasn't in control of things led her to personify money as an enemy.

That feeling is incredibly common.

I'll tell you what I told her: Money isn't alive. It doesn't have a brain. It certainly doesn't plot against you. It doesn't make decisions or hide behind corners waiting to ambush your checking account. Every dollar moves exactly the way you tell it to, consciously or not. Money isn't the enemy. The real challenge is in our behavior. If your money keeps disappearing, it's not because it ran off. It's because your habits led it out the door.

And that's good news.

IF YOU'RE NOT PART OF THE PROBLEM, YOU CAN'T BE PART OF THE SOLUTION.

If a genie came in and magically fixed your financial woes, you'd probably wind up right back where you started. Don't believe me? Ask lottery winners. A whopping 70 percent of people who win large sums of money in the lottery lose or spend it all within five years or less,[11] and 70 percent end up bankrupt.[12]

Take professional athletes as another example. By the time they have been retired for two years, 78 percent of former NFL players have gone bankrupt or are under financial stress because of joblessness or divorce. Within five years of retirement, an estimated 60 percent of former NBA players are broke.[13]

This suggests that no amount of wealth can protect a person from the inability to control spending. That control starts with you.

If your behavior is the problem, then your behavior can also be the solution. The key to financial success isn't outsmarting money, it's

---

11   Michael Crouch, "13 Things Lotto Winners Won't Tell You: Life After Winning the Lottery," *Reader's Digest*, March 15, 2024, https://www.rd.com/list/13-things-lottery-winners/.

12   Teresa Dixon Murray, "Why Do 70 Percent of Lottery Winners End Up Bankrupt?," cleveland.com, January 14, 2016, https://www.cleveland.com/business/2016/01/why_do_70_percent_of_lottery_w.html; Chris Gudgeon and Barbara Stewart, *Luck of the Draw: True-Life Tales of Lottery Winners and Losers* (Arsenal Pulp Press, 2002).

13   Pablo S. Torre, "How (and Why) Athletes Go Broke," *Sports Illustrated*, March 23, 2009, 23–35.

learning how to guide your own decisions more effectively, especially in the moments that matter most.

You also can't outsource this problem to a budgeting app, program, or plan. Not entirely, at least. The reality is that the right budgeting app can be a very powerful tool, but it is limited in what it can do. Ultimately, apps are just aids—they track your spending and maybe send you reminders about when you are close to overspending. While these are both helpful, they are no substitute for your own self-control.

So, first things first: Stop blaming the world and look in the mirror. The solution to your problem lies there.

TALKING TO YOUR ELEPHANT

I've talked a lot in this book about the importance of introspection. The purpose of honest introspection is to understand what the primitive elephant part of your brain wants. What tempts you? What are your weaknesses? What treats do you never allow yourself to buy, not because you dislike them but because you like them too much and eat them too fast? When and how do your completely natural human impulses step in to sabotage your long-term goals and objectives?

Your money personality, which you discovered in the quiz in Chapter 6, can give you insights into where to look for financial strengths and weaknesses. If you didn't complete the quiz earlier, go back and do so now.

Everyone will have a unique set of weaknesses and struggles, and these are the places where you need to focus your efforts. You need to be honest with yourself. This is not to shame you, but remember: You can't strengthen your weakness if you don't know what that weakness is to begin with.

In addition to identifying your vulnerable points, it is also critical to note what triggers these vulnerabilities. Does a stressful day at work prompt you to a spending spree? Do you buy tons of junk food every time you fight with your spouse or parents? If you really want to go hardcore, psychologists recommend that you keep a journal to note what happened in your life immediately prior to your feeling tempted to engage in a destructive financial behavior that you are trying to curb.

This self-reflection is also an ongoing process. As time goes on, you may find new areas of difficulty appearing while things that used to be difficult become easier. Keep an eye not only on your behaviors but on how you feel when engaging in these behaviors. This will be the key to recognizing any emotional needs the behavior fulfills, and therefore the key to finding less expensive or destructive ways to satisfy the need.

Remember, your elephant isn't your enemy. It's not some inner saboteur trying to ruin your life. It *is* you. It's your instincts, your emotions, your cravings, your joy. You love something because your elephant loves it. That's why it's not just misguided to try to silence your elephant—it's self-defeating.

My elephant, for example, loves Star Wars, Cheetos, and spending time with my wife. It absolutely hates working out. And honestly, that's okay. Any attempt I make to suppress my elephant—shame it, silence it, force it into submission—is really just an attempt to deny the very things that make life worth living. My ability to experience happiness *comes from* the elephant. That's its power.

The challenge is, the elephant only knows how to chase what feels good *right now*. It doesn't think ahead. It doesn't weigh trade-offs or build strategies. That doesn't mean the elephant is broken; it just wasn't built for this type of planning.

But if I want more of the things I truly love—not just in the moment, but over the long run—I need to help my elephant walk a path that leads to lasting joy, not just fleeting rewards. The key isn't control through force. It's guidance through understanding.

GUIDING THE ELEPHANT

Balancing present desires with future goals is the job of the rider: that logical, future-focused part of your mind that plans, prioritizes, and pauses to think. But the trick is that the best way to win that battle is to avoid fighting it at all. Don't rely on brute-force willpower to wrestle the elephant into submission. You'll lose more often than you'd like to admit, because the elephant is stronger, faster, and always ready to charge.

The real strategy isn't fighting temptation in the moment, it's *preventing* those moments from having power in the first place. That means changing the way you make decisions so that fewer of them fall under the elephant's control. The best techniques don't try to overpower the elephant; they work with its nature. And while there are countless ways to do that, nearly all effective approaches follow two core principles for guiding the elephant:

GUIDING PRINCIPLE 1: MAKE DECISIONS FOR THE FUTURE, NOT IN THE MOMENT.

Your elephant doesn't plan ahead. It only responds to what's right in front of it. The more decisions you make in advance—when your rider is alert and focused and your elephant couldn't care less—the fewer temptations you will face to break the plan.

GUIDING PRINCIPLE 2: DON'T MAKE DECISIONS WHEN YOUR RIDER IS DEPLETED.

The second guiding principle is just as important: Avoid making decisions when your rider is running low. When you're tired, hungry, anxious, sad, or even just overwhelmed from too many choices, your rider gets weak and the elephant takes over. That's why the old advice to never shop while hungry is so effective. Hunger weakens your rider and strengthens your elephant. The result? Snap spending. You overspend, grab junk you didn't plan to buy, and leave wondering what happened.

With these two principles in mind, let's look at some practical ways to manage the elephant more effectively and steer your decisions toward long-term success.

HOLD A WEEKLY FINANCIAL PLANNING SESSION

Once a week, take a few minutes to sit down and plan your upcoming expenses. What meals are we going to eat? What ingredients do we need? Is a grocery trip required? And if so, how much is left in the grocery budget, and how much of it are we planning to spend this week? Do the kids need clothes? What does the spending plan say we have available and how much of it do we want to use this week?

This simple weekly habit is a great example of Guiding Principle 1: Make decisions for the future, not in the moment. By deciding in advance, you avoid having to make spur-of-the-moment choices when your elephant is in control—especially in high-temptation zones like a grocery store or big-box retailer. Planning ahead gives your rider the chance to direct your spending with intention rather than emotion.

This approach also embraces Guiding Principle 2: Don't make decisions when your rider is depleted. By shifting the decision-making to a calmer, more focused moment when your rider is at full strength, weekly planning short-circuits the trap of buying impulsively through-out the week.

This isn't about micromanaging every dollar. It's about setting up decisions ahead of time, when your rider is in charge, so your elephant can just follow the plan.

IMPLEMENT A WAITING PERIOD

When considering a moderate expense, one of the most effective tools you can use is a waiting period. A waiting period is a rule you impose on yourself and/or your household that says you must wait a certain amount of time between having the idea to buy something and actually making the purchase.

This is effective at managing primal temptations from the elephant for two reasons.

First, it shifts the decision out of the moment, which keeps the elephant from taking the reins. The waiting period creates space between the emotional impulse and the actual purchase. That's Guiding Principle 1: Make decisions for the future, not in the moment. The second benefit is just as important: by waiting, you give your rider a chance to be fully resourced—well-rested, fed, calm, and clear-headed. That's Guiding Principle 2: Don't make decisions when your rider is depleted.

Many people use a simple twenty-four-hour rule: You can't buy anything (outside of essentials) without sleeping on it first. But there's no magic in the number twenty-four—it's just a starting point. You can tailor this approach to your situation. For example, when my wife and I were newly married and money was tight, we made a rule that any nonessential purchase over $50 had to be discussed, and we had to wait twenty-four hours. As our financial circumstances improved, we increased the limit to $100 with a twenty-four-hour wait, but we only had to consult each other on purchases over $200. We also have a rule where any expense over $1,000 has a waiting period of at least one week, if possible. (Sometimes emergencies don't let us wait, like the time our AC went out in the middle of the Arizona summer. No way we were waiting a week to fix that!)

These rules don't just curb impulsive spending. They're systems for managing the elephant. They give your rider time to take control, assess your plan, and decide if the expense is really worth it. Many purchases lose their appeal with just a little time and distance. That's not failure—it's smart elephant handling.

CREATE COMMITMENT DEVICES

Believe it or not, you can actually harness your elephant's impulsive nature and put it to work for you. The same instincts that often throw you off track can, with a little strategy, help keep you on it. One of the most powerful ways to do that is through a commitment device: a structure you set up in advance that holds you to your better intentions when the moment of temptation hits.

Unlike a weekly spending plan or a twenty-four-hour waiting rule (which are about making thoughtful choices outside of the moment of decision), a commitment device steps in during the moment of weakness. It's your backup system, your safety net, your mental reinforcements showing up when your rider is tired and your elephant is ready to charge.

Think of it like Gandalf in *The Two Towers*. He couldn't be there at the start of the battle for Helm's Deep, but he promised he'd return when they needed him most. And he did—arriving at dawn with reinforcements just as the enemy was breaking through and hope was running out. The timing wasn't about drama, it was about strategy. The bright light of the rising sun gave his riders the advantage they needed to turn the tide.

A commitment device works the same way. You're setting things up in advance—before the battle begins—so that help arrives exactly when your resolve is weakest. It's not about being stronger in the moment. It's about being smarter *before* the moment comes.

You know yourself well enough to expect that future-you might try to talk you into something. So you set out to trick yourself, in the best way possible, into not giving in to temptation when the moment arrives. That might mean automating your savings before you ever see the money, deleting shopping apps, or using prepaid debit cards to physically limit your spending. It might mean telling a friend you'll owe them $50 if you skip your budgeting session. Whatever form it takes, a good commitment device works with your elephant by making the path of least resistance lead to good choices rather than poor ones.

Here's a simple nonfinancial example. Let's say your goal is to wake up early, but you've been struggling. At night, waking up early seems like a good idea, but in the morning it just doesn't seem worth it. What do you do? You set an alarm! This is a very simple commitment device.

So you set your alarm, but when it goes off you cave to temptation and hit snooze, thereby missing your goal. The reason you lost the battle and hit snooze is because when you are groggy, the primitive regions of your brain are in charge and the rational rider who set the goal to wake up is still sleeping. This is why it takes great self-control to meet this goal.

You can improve your alarm clock commitment device by moving the alarm to the other side of the room. This forces you to physically get out of bed if you want to hit snooze. Physically getting out of bed wakes up the strategic regions of your brain and gives you a far better chance of staying up.

You can take the across-the-room alarm idea to the next level with a clever little invention: a robot alarm clock you have to *chase* to turn off. These rolling alarms literally launch themselves off your nightstand and start zooming around the room, blaring at full volume while you scramble out of bed to catch them.

It's a brilliant way to get the primitive and strategic parts of your brain working together instead of at odds. In that moment, every part of you, whether rational or emotional, wants the same thing: *make it stop*. People who use these alarm clocks often report that getting out of bed becomes effortless because the urgency overrides the usual morning sluggishness. And once you're up and moving, staying up becomes much easier.

We can do similar things with financial goals.

One simple and effective commitment device is to set up an automatic transfer to a savings account at a separate bank; ideally one without easy access through a mobile app or debit card. The idea is to move money out of your main checking account before you even see it, locking in the decision to save while your rider is still in charge. When the elephant comes looking to spend, the money just isn't there. The time and effort of retrieving it from a separate institution gives your rational brain time to reengage.

Another approach is to create a "spend-match" rule: Every time you buy a nonessential item like a meal out or a new pair of shoes, you agree to transfer the same amount into savings or investments. If you're willing to spend $50 on a nice dinner, you also need to be willing to put $50 toward your Roth IRA or emergency fund. This forces a pause and reframes the decision: Is the purchase really worth paying double—once for the purchase and again for the deposit into savings? It turns discretionary spending into an opportunity for building long-term wealth.

A more passive commitment device is a round-up savings program, offered by many banks and apps. Every time you make a purchase, the total is rounded up to the nearest dollar and the spare change is automatically transferred to savings. For example, if you spend $3.25, 75¢ goes into your savings account. It's painless and automatic—your elephant never even notices the money is gone, but your savings steadily grow.

Finally, you can enlist the help of an accountability buddy: someone you check in with regularly about your financial goals. For example, you might agree to send a weekly text updating them on whether you stayed within your budget or avoided impulse purchases. You can even up the stakes by adding a consequence: If you break your rule, you owe them $20, or you have to donate to a cause you don't support. It's a light-hearted way to raise the cost of failure and use social pressure to support your better instincts.

CREATE GOAL REMINDERS

A very gentle commitment device involves posting pictures that represent your goals on the bathroom mirror or fridge door. This gives your primitive brain something a little more tangible to focus on and can therefore reduce the temptation to jeopardize the goal. You might discover other types of visual cues that work for you. The purpose is to allow the elephant to connect with your goal visually, and perhaps get it excited to participate.

My wife experienced this herself. When we were first married, I was the one who would move the money over from our checking account to our emergency fund each month; watch the balance grow; and mentally check it off the list. But at some point we decided to switch things up and my wife started making the transfers instead of me. Now let me be clear: My wife is not a big spender by any stretch. But between the two of us, I've always been the more natural saver.

What surprised us both was how much she loved it. She started watching the balance climb with real excitement. She'd tell me things like "I was about to buy something today, but then I imagined transferring that money to the emergency fund instead, and that just felt better." For her, seeing that number go up became its own kind of reward.

That was a powerful shift. What changed wasn't just her behavior—it was true elephant buy-in. Her emotional brain, the part that normally resists saving because it lacks an immediate payoff, actually *wanted* to save. She began to feel excited watching the balance grow in real time. Before then, saving was something she did because it was the smart, responsible choice. It made sense and aligned with our goals. But once she took over the transfers, it stopped feeling like a chore and started feeling like something she genuinely *enjoyed*.

That's the sweet spot: when a decision that fits your strategy and moves you toward your goals doesn't feel like an obligation and actually feels good. The rider might set the plan, but the elephant needs to enjoy the ride (or at least the view). You won't always get to that point, but when you do, it's incredibly powerful. I tried to harness this same effect to get myself to the gym. I created a progress chart and promised myself rewards if I could exercise regularly enough to fill in the chart.

That motivational system failed completely. I just didn't care about whether the chart was filled in or not. For some people, tracking progress visually is deeply satisfying—it lights up their elephant, makes them feel accomplished, and keeps them moving. But for me? It was just another thing to ignore. A filled-in chart didn't feel like a reward. It felt like homework.

And that's the thing: what motivates *your* elephant may be very different from what motivates mine. You can't just assume a system that works for someone else is going to work for you. Some elephants get excited by progress bars and sticker charts. Others respond better to physical discomfort, social accountability, or the thrill of earning a reward. That's why it's worth experimenting with goal reminders. Try a few different approaches and pay close attention not just to whether they work, but to how they *feel*.

Maybe a visual tracker doesn't motivate you, but a concrete commitment device does. For example, you might decide not to replace your saggy, uncomfortable couch until you've paid off your car loan. Every time you sit down and feel that lumpy cushion, you're reminded of the bigger goal. The discomfort becomes a cue: your elephant doesn't like it, and that mild frustration can actually help fuel your follow-through. You're giving your emotional brain a reason to care.

Or maybe you need something more external, like a friend you check in with once a week or a public commitment that raises the stakes. You might find that your elephant loves watching a savings account grow but couldn't care less about hitting an abstract percentage of your retirement target. Or maybe it's the opposite.

TREAT YOURSELF

Building on the idea of using visual reminders or discomfort as cues, you can also flip the approach and actively *reward* your elephant for taking small, intentional steps in the right direction. This turns progress into a source of immediate satisfaction, which is exactly what your elephant craves.

The key here is to make the reward feel meaningful without undermining your financial goals, so think small, inexpensive, and genuinely enjoyable.

For example, if you stick to your grocery budget for the week, let yourself pick out a candy bar you love. If you skip a takeout meal and cook at home instead, maybe you earn a guilt-free hour watching your favorite show or scrolling TikTok. The point isn't to bribe yourself with something extravagant; it's to create a clear, emotional payoff that makes the right behavior feel good *now*, not just someday in the future.

I call these little rewards *elephant treats*—small but powerful nudges that build momentum. They reinforce the habit loop: trigger, action, reward. The elephant remembers what felt good, and it becomes more likely to follow that path again.

What works as a reward will be different for everyone. For some, it's a piece of chocolate. For others, it's lighting a candle they love, sipping a favorite drink, or even just checking off a box on a fun-looking habit tracker. It doesn't have to be fancy. It just has to feel *real* to your emotional brain.

The trick is consistency. Set the rules in advance so your rider is in charge of the structure, and then follow through so your elephant gets the reward. Over time, these small reinforcements can retrain your elephant to associate saving, budgeting, or restraint with something positive. And once that happens, you've done more than make a good decision—you've created a system your whole brain wants to keep following.

USE AUTOMATIC DEPOSIT

This tip is my personal favorite and the most powerful of the bunch. The idea here is that you simply bypass your ability to be tempted by automating your finances as much as possible.

By setting up an automatic transfer from your checking account to your savings or investment account, you allocate funds to your goals before you're tempted to spend them. This "pay yourself first" approach ensures that a portion of your income is consistently saved, helping you steadily progress towards savings goals like emergency funds, retirement, or paying off debt.

Automating this process removes the mental burden of manual transfers, and it keeps your savings plan on track effortlessly. You don't have to fight the temptation to spend, because you have no money to spend. This approach may require you to cancel your credit cards and just use debit cards. And, of course, you are still going to have to monitor your spending. But even if you do spend all the money in your checking account, your savings account can remain untouched.

The money in your savings account should be held in a different bank from your day-to-day checking account. This separation creates a psychological barrier that can deter impulsive withdrawals and spending. In fact, the savings accounts that will pay the most interest will often have restrictions on when and how fast you can withdraw your money. Even the fastest transfers can take a few days. This built-in lag between when you request the money and when you receive it gives you a chance to cool down and make a planned, rather than impulsive, decision.

When your savings are not immediately visible or accessible during your regular banking activities, it reduces the temptation to dip into these funds for nonessential purchases. Additionally, having a separate savings account can often provide better interest rates or savings incentives, optimizing your savings growth over time. This approach reinforces the commitment to your financial goals, making it a powerful strategic move.

JENNA BREAKS HER SPENDING LOOP

You might remember Jenna: the student who realized she'd been stuck in a snap-spending loop, buying small things like candles and water bottles whenever she felt stressed or unsettled. She wasn't spending for function—she was spending for feeling. And once she saw that pattern, she knew she needed more than just awareness. She needed a system. So she set one up.

Jenna created a separate savings account at a different bank—one that didn't offer a debit card or an app—and arranged for a portion of each paycheck to be automatically deposited there before she ever saw it in her main checking account. It wasn't a huge amount, but it was enough to disrupt the old pattern and build a new one.

"I realized my default was to spend whenever I felt off," she said. "My elephant kept chasing a quick hit of happiness. Something to feel better in the moment. But it never lasted. I needed a new default, one that gave my rider a little more control."

By making the money harder to access, she removed the immediate option to spend. And that pause—just a little distance between impulse and action—was often enough to shift the decision. It wasn't about depriving herself; it was about changing the script.

Over time, Jenna didn't just save more. She found better ways to respond to the feelings that used to trigger spending. She started taking walks, journaling, reaching out to friends and doing other things that actually helped her feel better in a lasting way. She stopped trying to buy peace of mind and instead started building it.

YOUR UNIQUE SOLUTION

Ultimately, none of these things may work for you. The single greatest challenge of personal financial planning is that it's just that—personal. What works for one person may not work for another. What motivates me may not motivate you. Everyone has to experiment to learn their own personal quirks, temptations, weaknesses, and strengths that are revealed in their money personality. Don't be shy about exploring methods and trying new tools in your quest for financial self-mastery!

Guiding your elephant isn't about finding the perfect strategy on the first try. It's about learning how *your* elephant responds—what excites it, what spooks it, what keeps it moving in the direction you actually want to go. The best financial systems aren't just aligned with your goals; they're aligned with your nature. They work *with* your instincts, not against them.

Each of us is unique. So listen closely to the messages your elephant is sending you. You can get some insight from your money personality, but your elephant will also talk directly to you. Its messages don't come as neatly labeled advice—they show up as feelings, thoughts, and impulses. What are you feeling in the moment? What is that feeling pushing you to do? That's your elephant talking to your rider. The more attuned you become to those signals, the better you'll be at guiding your decisions; not by brute force, but by insight.

So try things. Pay attention. Adjust. Some strategies will click right away. Others will flop completely. That's not failure—it's feedback. My gym progress chart didn't work, but that doesn't mean I'm lazy or undisciplined. It just means that that method didn't speak to my elephant. So I tried something else: finding games that require physical exertion, but which my elephant doesn't recognize as "exercise"; and by intentionally making routine tasks more energy intensive, like climbing the stairs instead of taking the elevator or curling grocery bags as I bring them in from the car. My fitness routine is still a work in progress, but I have made improvements, and that's what's most important.

Every misfire is just more information. Don't give up. Use that information to learn and improve your strategy. Over time, you'll build a toolbox filled with strategies that work for *you*—strategies that move you forward without constant resistance. The goal isn't to fight your elephant. The goal is to understand it well enough to lead it.

MOMENTS OF CLARITY

- **Financial success starts with behavior change.** No amount of income or wealth can compensate for poor spending habits. Without self-awareness and structure, even lottery winners and professional athletes can go broke.

- **Your elephant isn't your enemy—it is *you*.** It's your emotions, impulses, and instincts. The goal isn't to silence it, but to guide it with understanding and structure.

- **Simple systems work best.** Weekly planning sessions, waiting periods for purchases, and visual cues can reduce impulsive decisions and help your rider stay in control.

- **Experiment and observe.** Pay attention to what motivates or derails you. Your elephant has preferences—figure out what they are and build systems that work with them.

CHAPTER NINE

A STRATEGY FOR EMPOWERED SPENDING

You've built a vision for what you want. Maybe it's a secure retirement, travel, time with family, launching your own business, or being free from debt. You've thought about your values. You've reflected on your priorities. Now comes the part where those ideas become real: how you use your money *today*.

It's tempting to think of saving and investing as the heart of your financial strategy. But really, spending is the engine. It's the part that happens every day. And it's the part you control. If your spending isn't aligned with your vision, nothing else will get you where you want to go.

That's why empowered spending sits at the center of this framework.

Empowered spending means taking control; intentionally directing your dollars so they contribute to the life you want. Not just someday in the future, but today too. It's about making each paycheck pull double duty: funding a life you enjoy now while building the life you're working toward. It's spending that empowers you to live the life you most enjoy both now *and* later.

And that starts by knowing what actually brings you joy. When you pause to look closely at your spending—really look—you'll notice something: Not all dollars deliver the same amount of happiness. Sometimes it fades fast. Other times the happiness stays with you. Empowered spending grows from that awareness. It requires us to ask, *Which expenses consistently make my life better? Which ones don't?*

STRATEGY IS THE CORE

This is exactly why you took the time to build a strategy. Your strategy starts with your vision: what you want your money to accomplish. It clarifies your values, defines your goals, and gives you a filter for sorting your spending: *Does this help me build the life I want, or does it pull me further from it?*

That clarity is everything. Without a strategy, a spending plan is just a list of numbers. It becomes reactive; focused on cutting or controlling rather than creating and directing. You might be tracking where your money went, but you're not telling it where to go.

Your strategy is what gives your spending plan purpose. It's the *why* behind every dollar. It tells you what deserves funding before you ever sit down to allocate your paycheck. And once you're clear on that, the rest becomes much easier: You're not budgeting out of guilt or fear, you're simply aligning your money with the life you have decided that you want.

Too often, people hear the word "budget" and immediately associate it with suffering—cutting out lattes, saying no to fun, denying joy. But that's the opposite of what an empowered spending plan should do.

A good spending strategy isn't about restriction. It's about making space: for joy, for progress, for peace of mind. It lets you stop wasting money on things that don't matter so you can spend more boldly on what does. The power of a strategy-driven plan is that it puts you in control—not just of your money, but of your life.

CREATE A SPENDING STRATEGY THAT EMPOWERS YOU

Once you have your overall vision and direction in place, you can start crafting strategies for different areas of your finances. And when it comes to day-to-day spending decisions, that means creating a spending strategy.

Constantly pausing to evaluate every purchase is exhausting. Nobody does this all the time. We just don't have the time or energy. That's why we need tools and shortcuts to make mindful spending easier, more automatic, and less draining. A good spending strategy does exactly that. It provides a clear, practical framework that guides your daily choices with less effort and more confidence.

While the biggest financial decisions still deserve careful thought, your everyday spending can be dramatically simplified with a strategy in place. A spending strategy is not your budget or even a detailed plan for spending. It's the bridge between your long-term vision and your short-term budget. It gives your spending purpose and direction without the rigidity that makes traditional budgeting feel like punishment.

> A SPENDING STRATEGY IS THE
> BRIDGE BETWEEN YOUR VISION
> AND YOUR DAILY BUDGET.

Think of it like any other strategy—it keeps you oriented toward your goals. It helps you navigate the countless little choices you face each week while staying aligned with what matters most. It balances the discipline required for financial security with the freedom to enjoy the present. And when life doesn't go according to plan, your strategy still gives you direction, so you can adapt without losing your footing.

BUILD YOUR SPENDING STRATEGY

Creating a spending strategy means translating your financial vision into daily decisions you can actually stick to. It's not about building the perfect spreadsheet—it's about building a system that helps you make smarter choices without burning out. A good strategy reduces friction, cuts through noise, and gives your rational self a fighting chance before your emotional elephant decides you *definitely need* that limited-edition espresso machine. At its core, your spending strategy has three key components:

I. BROAD GUIDELINES FOR SPENDING CATEGORIES

Start by sketching out which types of spending deserve a spotlight, which deserve a dimmer switch, and which can be shown the door entirely. These are your big-picture rules that keep your spending aligned with your values. Maybe you want to invest more in housing and education, while cutting back on brand-name splurges or trimming your ever-growing stack of forgotten subscriptions. These aren't hard limits—they're directional signals, helping you say *yes* with confidence and *no* without regret.

2. PLANS FOR MANAGING TEMPTATIONS AND RELATIONSHIPS

Let's be honest: Your biggest financial leaks probably won't come from overspending on groceries, they'll come from impulse buys, social pressure, and emotional mood boosters. That's why part of your strategy should include guardrails for those moments when the elephant wants to charge. This might mean setting a "fun money" allowance, using a 24-hour pause rule for nonessentials, or agreeing with your partner on shared spending goals so money talks don't turn into money fights. It's about being honest with yourself and building in just enough flexibility to keep your strategy human-proof.

3. GUIDELINES FOR MANAGING CASH ON HAND

Cash doesn't just offer peace of mind—it buys you leverage. With a solid cash reserve you can handle emergencies without running to your credit card and avoid financing charges on those mid-sized "life happens" expenses. Your strategy should define how much you want in your emergency fund, how you'll build it, and the rules for when it's okay to dip into it. This isn't just about discipline. It's about designing a system that protects your progress and gives you the freedom to act with confidence when opportunity (or crisis) comes knocking.

Done right, your spending strategy isn't a burden—it's a relief. It saves your brain from decision fatigue, reins in your inner elephant, and lets you live more intentionally with less stress.

Let's turn now to see how one family puts these principles into practice.

THE THOMPSON FAMILY'S SPENDING STRATEGY

Meet the Thompson family—a family of four living in a suburban community in the United States. As you'll see, their financial vision provides the why, their spending strategy offers the how, and their spending plan lays out the steps needed to bring their goals to life.

FAMILY MEMBERS:

- John (38) and Sarah (36): Parents working in mid-level professional roles. John is a project manager for a tech company and Sarah is a teacher.

- Emma (10) and Noah (7): John and Sarah's children; attending elementary school.

CURRENT FINANCIAL SITUATION:

- Annual Household Income: $120,000

- Monthly Expenses: $7,000 (including housing, utilities, groceries, and childcare)

- Savings: $25,000 in an emergency fund, $40,000 in retirement accounts

- Debt: $15,000 remaining on a car loan at 4 percent interest, $5,000 in credit card debt at 18 percent interest

THE THOMPSON FAMILY'S FINANCIAL VISION

CORE VALUES:

- Family Time: They prioritize spending quality time together, especially through shared activities and vacations.

- Education: Ensuring their children have access to excellent educational opportunities is nonnegotiable.

- Security: Maintaining financial stability and preparing for the unexpected are key priorities.

GOALS:

- **Short-Term Goals (1–2 Years):**
    - Pay off the $5,000 in credit card debt.
    - Build an additional $5,000 into their emergency fund to cover six months of expenses.
    - Take a modest family vacation to Yellowstone National Park, budgeting $4,000.

- **Medium-Term Goals (3–5 Years):**
    - Save $20,000 for Emma's and Noah's extracurricular activities and summer camps.
    - Replace the family car for around $30,000 and aim to minimize financing charges by saving for a significant down payment.

- **Long-Term Goals (10+ Years):**
    - Save $150,000 for their children's college education.
    - Pay off their mortgage early to reduce financial obligations before retirement.
    - Retire at 60 with a retirement fund of $1.5 million.

THE THOMPSONS CREATE
A SPENDING STRATEGY

The Thompsons' spending strategy serves as their guide for making intentional financial decisions that align with their family's vision. They aren't just trying to stay on budget—they're trying to build a life that reflects what matters most to them. Their vision is rooted in a set of clearly defined core values: security, connection, growth, and generosity. From that foundation, they've mapped out their short-, medium-, and long-term goals, including a stable home life, memorable family experiences, a strong retirement, and support for their children's education and development.

But before diving into specific budget categories and dollar amounts, the Thompsons recognized the need for a set of general principles—guidelines that help them evaluate trade-offs and direct their income in a way that serves both today's joy and tomorrow's goals. These guidelines act like a compass: not rigid rules, but steady reference points that keep them oriented toward the life they want to build.

They asked themselves, *What spending consistently adds to our happiness and well-being? What kinds of expenses fade quickly and leave us wanting more? And where can we get the same joy for less?*

The guidelines that arose from these questions are a critical part of their strategy because they give the Thompsons flexibility. No month ever goes exactly according to plan—unexpected expenses pop up, things change, life happens. But instead of scrambling in the moment, they've already thought through how they want to respond. They know what they're willing to cut and what they'll allow themselves to splurge on when the opportunity is worth it. That foresight proactively turns the chaotic moments of the upcoming month into a series of chances to choose from just a few preselected options. Foresight allows them to act as the rational rider, guiding their financial decisions rather than being pulled off course by the emotional elephant.

After some consideration, the Thompsons decide on the following spending strategy:

1. Spending they prioritize because it reflects their values and brings consistent joy:

    a. They make space in their budget for activities that build family connection. That includes a weekly tradition of going out for Saturday breakfast together—a relatively small expense that anchors their weekend and gives everyone something to look forward to. They also budget year-round for experiences, like day trips and holiday outings, so they can create shared memories without financial stress.

    b. Education is another top priority. They regularly invest in their kids' learning and growth, setting aside funds for things like books, learning apps, extracurricular activities, and enrichment programs. Even small costs like museum memberships or science kits get a green light if they support Emma and Noah's development.

    c. And because security is central to their vision, the Thompsons make room for peace-of-mind spending. That includes things like regular car maintenance to avoid costly breakdowns later or paying a little extra for quality home insurance. They view these not as boring necessities, but as tools to protect what they're building.

2. Spending they enjoy but intentionally limit or manage:

    a. Dining out is something the Thompsons like, but they've realized it can quickly eat into their budget without delivering lasting value. So instead of cutting it entirely, they treat restaurant nights as a planned indulgence: twice a month, at places they truly enjoy. That way it feels like a treat, not a habit.

b.   They've also noticed that impulse purchases, especially for home decor and clothing, tend to offer short-lived satisfaction. Now they keep wish lists and revisit them monthly. If something still feels worthwhile, they'll make room for it in the plan. If not, they let it go.

c.   Subscriptions and streaming services are another area they monitor closely. While they value family movie nights and some on-demand entertainment, they've learned to avoid the trap of accumulating too many subscriptions. They do regular reviews to cancel anything that's no longer getting used.

d.   By consistently spending in line with their values of family, education, and security, the Thompsons don't just manage their money. They use it to create a life that feels both joyful and purposeful, today and tomorrow.

3.   Spending they intentionally avoid because it doesn't align with their values or deliver enough return for the cost:

a.   The Thompsons have identified status spending as a category they actively steer clear of. They've realized that trying to keep up with neighbors or coworkers—whether that means upgrading to the latest tech, buying designer clothes, or choosing luxury brands—doesn't add real value to their lives. These purchases tend to be expensive, fleeting, and disconnected from the things they truly care about.

b.   For them, spending money to impress others is one of the quickest ways to drain resources that could instead be used to build lasting security or create meaningful experiences for their family. They've agreed that when something feels like it's more about appearance than impact, it's not worth the price tag.

Spending They Prioritize	Spending They Limit	Spending They Avoid
Weekly family breakfasts	Dining out more than twice a month	Designer or brand-name fashion
Day trips and shared experiences	Home decor or clothing purchases	Latest tech gadgets without clear need
Books and educational resources	Multiple streaming subscriptions	Luxury vehicles or home upgrades for status
Kids' extracurricular activities	Convenience snacks and drinks	Purchases made to impress others
Preventive maintenance and insurance		

TABLE 9.1

DEBT MANAGEMENT

The Thompsons are focused on eliminating high-interest debt as a foundational step toward financial security. Their top priority is to pay off their $5,000 credit card balance within the next year. In addition, they're continuing regular payments on their car loan, aiming to have it fully paid off within two years. This will free up additional monthly cash flow they can then redirect toward savings and other goals.

They've also committed to avoiding new consumer debt unless absolutely necessary, reinforcing their value of long-term stability.

SAVINGS GUIDELINES

To maintain their sense of financial security and support their long-term vision, the Thompsons have clear savings targets. They keep at least $20,000 in their emergency fund, enough to cover two months of essential expenses. They contribute $250 each month toward their children's educational and extracurricular needs, reflecting their strong commitment to supporting Emma's and Noah's development.

To stay on track for their retirement goal of $1.5 million, they've automated $1,000 in monthly contributions to their retirement accounts, treating savings like a nonnegotiable bill rather than an afterthought.

THE IMPORTANCE OF A FINANCIAL VISION

A key component of the Thompsons' strategy (particularly the financial compass) is removing the need to resist spending temptations in the moment. By deciding ahead of time what their spending priorities are—and perhaps more importantly, what they are not—the Thompsons make it easier to stick to their plan. The vision and spending plan also provide motivation for exercising discipline in spending, as they give distinct reasons for why certain sacrifices are worth making. For instance, the Thompsons want to take a family vacation to Yellowstone. Knowing this, they are more likely to skip impulse buys and instead focus on their goal. They understand that every dollar saved brings them closer to success. (To remind them of this goal, they might put a photo of Old Faithful on their fridge and ask the kids to remind them that they're supposed to be saving for Yellowstone, not buying another lamp.)

By prioritizing their values, managing debt strategically, and planning ahead, the Thompsons can achieve financial stability while enjoying a fulfilling family life. Their financial vision provides the why, their spending strategy offers the how, and their spending plan delivers the actionable steps needed to bring their goals to life. This comprehensive approach allows them to navigate challenges with confidence and purpose, building a secure and meaningful future.

MOMENTS OF CLARITY

- **Empowered spending** is intentional spending: using your money in ways that support both the life you enjoy now and the future you're working toward.

- **A spending strategy is not a strict budget.** It's a flexible framework that bridges long-term goals and short-term choices, reducing stress and decision fatigue.

- **Set broad guidelines for spending categories.** Decide what you'll prioritize, limit, or avoid so you can act with clarity instead of impulse.

- **Build a plan to manage temptation.** Use your spending guidelines to decide in advance where you might cut back if necessary, and where you might spend more if things go well.

CHAPTER TEN

BUILDING A SPENDING PLAN

J ames sat across from me, frustration written all over his face. His case-study notes were covered in highlighter and margin scribbles, and his spreadsheet contained at least six versions of a monthly budget.

"I just need to know how much he's *supposed* to spend on rent," he said, tapping the table. "Is thirty percent too much or not? I feel like there should be a number."

I smiled. "It depends."

He threw his pen down. "That's not helpful! You gave me a fictional client and now you won't even tell me the right answer."

But here's the thing: I wasn't dodging the question. I was giving him the real answer. There *is* no magic percentage. His fictional client had $700 a month in student loans, a goal to open a food truck in three years, and was still driving a car held together with duct tape and hope. Whether spending 30 percent of his income on rent is too much depends entirely on what else matters in his life.

That's the moment this chapter is built for.

You've already done the hard work of building your strategy, defining what really matters to you and what kind of life you want to build. Now it's time to make that real. Not by plugging your income into a formula, but by creating a spending plan that reflects your actual priorities.

I call it a spending plan because it's not a one-size-fits-all budget or a guilt trip disguised as a spreadsheet. It's a plan that helps you get the most from your money by aligning it with what matters most to you.

The goal here isn't restriction. It's clarity. It's empowerment. It's about setting up a system that helps you spend boldly on the best parts of life and gently say no to the rest.

POPULAR SPENDING PLAN STRUCTURES

So how do you actually figure out if your spending lines up with your goals?

There's no one-size-fits-all answer, but there *are* some useful tools that can help you get your bearings. What follows are three common approaches people use to build a spending plan. They're not commandments, and none of them are perfect. In fact, I've spent decades exploring financial rules of thumb for budgeting, and I haven't found a single one that always works.

Think of these as starting points rather than rules. Try one on. See how it fits. If it doesn't work for your situation, try another, or adapt it until it does fit. Your spending plan should work for you, not the other way around.

Let's look at three different frameworks you can use.

FIXED-EXPENSES FOCUS

This approach starts with a simple idea: If your fixed expenses eat up too much of your income, everything else—your goals, your flexibility, your fun—gets squeezed out.

That's why this framework puts fixed expenses front and center. It helps you draw a line before commitments like rent, car payments, or subscriptions quietly take over your budget. The most popular version of this method is the **50/20/30 rule**:

- **Fifty percent** of your income goes to *fixed needs*—things like housing, transportation, utilities, insurance.

- **Twenty percent** is reserved for *financial goals*—saving, investing, paying off debt.

- **Thirty percent** is left for *wants*—everything from takeout to travel to that concert you just have to see.

The strength of this method is its built-in pressure test. Thinking about upgrading your apartment or buying a new car? Plug in the numbers. If that new monthly payment pushes your fixed expenses past 50 percent, that's a red flag.

Unlike some budgeting systems that focus on tracking every latte, this one zooms out. It gives you breathing room, but only after you've locked down those fixed costs. The more you can trim your fixed commitments, the more freedom you create in the rest of your life.

Let's look at this framework in greater detail:

Fixed Expenses (50 Percent of Income)

Allocate about 50 percent of your income to fixed expenses. These are often essential needs like housing, utilities, groceries, and transportation.

However, fixed expenses can also be more discretionary, like gym memberships or loan payments. The key feature of fixed expenses is that (1) they are a similar amount each month and (2) they repeat—usually monthly, though some expenses (like auto or life insurance premiums) come just once per quarter or once per year.

The relative inflexibility of fixed expenses makes them an important cornerstone of your overall spending patterns, which is why this approach focuses on them first.

Fifty percent is the typical amount set aside for fixed expenses, but you don't have to stick to that. Your chosen percentage may vary based on your location and lifestyle, but keeping fixed expenses within defined limits helps ensure you have enough money left over for the fun stuff, as well as for meeting your financial goals.

Financial Goals (20 Percent of Income)

Around 20 percent of your income should go towards meeting financial goals, such as debt repayment, accumulating an emergency fund, and investing for retirement. This allocation is crucial for long-term financial health. It's the glue that holds your financial foundations together. Don't neglect it. You should have long-term financial goals in your vision and as part of your spending strategy. This 20 percent is there to ensure you are making progress on these parts of your greater financial strategy.

Discretionary Spending (30% of Income)

The remaining 30 percent of your income can be used for discretionary spending, which includes entertainment, dining out, travel, hobbies, and other nonessential items.

This approach strikes a solid middle ground on flexibility. It's not as rigid as a line-item budget, but it's not a free-for-all either. The key is that it anchors your spending plan around fixed expenses—the part of your budget that's hardest to change once it's set.

By keeping those fixed costs within limits, you preserve flexibility elsewhere. You create space to adjust your lifestyle spending and financial goals without being boxed in by oversized monthly commitments. It's a smart trade-off: focus discipline where it matters most so the rest of your budget can breathe.

And while the 50/20/30 breakdown is the most well-known version of this method, it's just one way to frame it. You can shift the numbers to better fit your situation. Maybe 45/25/30 makes more sense for your life right now. That's fine as long as you're not starving your long-term goals. Cut too much from that 20 percent and you risk drifting farther from the stability and freedom you're trying to build.

The trade-off? You'll likely need to track and total things up yourself. Some budgeting apps can help, but depending on how they label categories, you might need to do a little manual sorting to get things aligned the way you want. It's a bit more hands-on, but for many people, the flexibility is worth it.

JENNA'S FIXED-EXPENSES FRAMEWORK: FLIPPING TO 50/30/20

My former student Jenna told me that she adopted a fixed-expenses framework. After reviewing a few months of her spending, Jenna discovered that not only were her fixed expenses a little high, but she also wasn't saving consistently, and her credit card balance had crept higher than she realized. So instead of the standard 50/20/30 split, she decided to flip the script—putting 30 percent of her income toward debt payments and savings and limiting her "wants" category to just 20 percent.

It was a temporary shift, but a powerful one. She automated everything:

- Ten percent straight into her retirement account
- Fifteen percent to aggressively pay down her credit card
- Five percent into that separate, hard-to-access savings account for emergencies

The remaining 50 percent went to fixed needs, and her "fun money" was capped at 20 percent. That tighter limit helped her stay conscious of her snap-spending urges, but because she had already handled her savings and goals, she didn't feel deprived—just more in control.

"The structure gave me momentum," she told me. "It felt like I was finally catching up instead of falling behind."

After a couple years of sticking to the more aggressive 50/30/20 plan, Jenna paid off her credit card completely and built up a small emergency fund. With those goals met, she loosened things up a bit, shifting to a more traditional 50/20/30 split that gave her more breathing room for travel, treats, and yes, the occasional candle.

The real shift wasn't just in her numbers. It was in her mindset. She no longer spent to escape discomfort, and she had a system that reflected her priorities. Her money was no longer reacting to her emotions. It was serving her goals.

That's the power of adapting your plan to your season of life. Sometimes speed is the goal. Sometimes, balance. Either way, it starts with intention.

THE SAVINGS FOCUS PLAN

If the fixed-expense strategy feels a little too rigid, the savings-first approach might suit you better. One of the most straightforward versions is the 80/20 plan: allocate 20 percent of your income to saving, debt repayment (excluding long-term fixed debts like a mortgage or auto loan), and future financial goals—then do whatever you want with the remaining 80 percent.

The key idea? *Protect your future first.* Once that 20 percent is set aside, the rest is yours to manage as you see fit.

This approach flips the usual budgeting script. Instead of scrutinizing every category or tracking fixed versus variable expenses, it puts all the focus on ensuring that your long-term financial stability is covered. That's the nonnegotiable part. Everything else? Up to you.

What makes this work so well is automation. Rather than relying on willpower, you can route your paycheck so the 20 percent is automatically divided and sent where it needs to go:

- Ten percent into your 401(k) or Roth IRA

- Five percent toward credit card or other short-term debt

- Five percent into a high-yield savings account for emergencies or future opportunities

The remaining 80 percent lands in your checking account, and you're free to spend it however you like—no guilt, no daily budget math, no tracking receipts. You're living within your means and building wealth in the background.

This method is ideal for people who value simplicity and flexibility but still want to be responsible with their future. Just one word of caution: If you tend to overspend or lose track of your cash flow, that 80 percent can disappear quickly. Without some awareness or guardrails, you might end up borrowing from tomorrow to pay for today, undermining the very goals you set out to protect. Still, when used intentionally, the savings-first strategy is one of the easiest and most sustainable ways to build lasting financial security without micromanaging your life.

This is the method I use myself. I automatically send a large chunk of my income into a combination of accounts: my emergency fund, short-term savings goals, and retirement savings. What's left stays in my checking account and I spend from there without micromanaging categories. It works beautifully for me, because I hate feeling like money is controlling me, so tedious tracking feels like a nightmare. Add to that the fact that I'm a compulsive saver who hates spending, and the risk of overspending just isn't a concern. So this is the perfect spending plan structure for me.

THE DOLLAR FOCUS (OR ZERO-BASED BUDGETING)

This approach is all about details. In a dollar-focused plan, every dollar gets a job and is expected to stick to it. You plan $500 for groceries, $25 for streaming, $300 for gas. You don't just hope your spending aligns with your goals; you *design* it to.

This method, often called zero-based budgeting, is a favorite for people who crave clarity and control. If you love spreadsheets, categorization, and the satisfaction of knowing exactly where every dollar went, this is your plan. It offers total visibility and total accountability, and for the right person, that's incredibly empowering.

Case in point: my old college roommate, Randy. Randy is 100 percent a zero-based budgeter. He tracks every expense down to the penny and genuinely enjoys the process. He's got color-coded spreadsheets, budget meetings with himself, and monthly spending reviews that would rival a corporate finance team. There were times when it made me tired just watching him go through his detailed budgeting process.

To be honest, I have no doubt that, in total, Randy's spending is more efficient than mine. He squeezes value from each dollar precisely because he's built a system that plays to his strengths and personality. Despite the substantial differences in our approaches, both work extremely well. His system meets his goals and works for him while my system meets my goals and works for me. That's the point.

Zero-based budgeting is powerful, but only if it fits the way you think and live.

If you're not naturally detail oriented, this approach can feel like a second job. Many people dive in with good intentions but give up within a few months because the system feels too rigid or time-consuming. That's not a failure, it's just a mismatch. And it's why, after trying this method too soon, many people swear off budgeting entirely. Don't let that be you.

That said, if you thrive on structure and want to really understand your money, this can be an amazing tool. Just know it requires a robust tracking system—either through a top-tier budgeting app or a serious commitment to manual updates. Even the best software will occasionally miscategorize expenses, so you'll still need to check in regularly and keep things on track.

One important caveat: zero-based budgeting tells you how to manage your money, but not what to prioritize. It won't help you decide how much to spend on rent versus groceries, or whether you're saving enough. You can—and probably should—pair it with your spending strategy, and another framework like 50/20/30 or 80/20 for guiding your higher-level allocations. Then use the zero-based budgeting method to break down your discretionary bucket into detailed categories for greater control and insight.

THE IMPORTANCE OF MONITORING

Why bother monitoring your spending? Because it's far too easy to completely lose track of how much you have spent in any given month, so monitoring is crucial for ensuring that you stay on track toward your financial goals. To monitor successfully, you've got to regularly check in on your financial habits to make sure they align with the priorities and limits you've set.

You might have guessed that tracking is important for making sure that you are following your spending plan accurately. If so, then you are correct. However, there is another, even more important reason to track your spending; one that is almost never discussed.

Tracking your expenses gives you insight into the life you are building with your spending. This is critical because the usual pattern of our spending does not contribute to our long-term goals; we have to consciously choose to make it do that. Without an intentional approach to our spending, we humans tend to spend by instinct. We spend on what we see in front of us, fulfilling wants and needs as they arise. Unfortunately, our basic neurobiology pushes us towards a focus on the present, which causes us to spend disproportionately on things that ultimately are not high priorities. In other words, monitoring our spending shows us where our spending is not meeting our highest priorities and desires!

Everyone who starts tracking their spending will eventually have an "I spent how much on *what!?*" moment. And that's okay.

It's not a matter of discipline. It's not a matter of strength or virtue. The evolutionary history that created our modern human brains pushes us to this behavior. No one is exempt from the influence of the primal elephant in our brain. The existence of surprises in your spending patterns isn't truly important in the grand scheme of things. What matters is that you commit to making adjustments as needed. Do that, and you'll eventually find yourself reaching your financial goals.

Perfection is not the goal of a spending plan. No one is perfect and no spending plan has ever been executed perfectly in the history of humankind. The important thing is to not break your spending plan *every* month. The occasional expensive month isn't the end of the world if you are generally being consistent in following your spending plan.

Here's how you can effectively monitor your expenses:

1. TRACK YOUR SPENDING REGULARLY

The first step in monitoring your expenses is to track them consistently. Most people prefer doing this through one of literally thousands of budgeting apps that automatically categorize and track your spending. These apps provide real-time updates on how your spending aligns with your budget. Such apps are popular because they provide the easiest and most streamlined experiences for tracking expenses.

However, this type of app is not the only option. Some people prefer a more hands-on approach. They download their bank and credit card statements, upload them into a spreadsheet such as Excel or Google Sheets, and run the numbers themselves.

Regardless of your approach, you absolutely must have a method for tracking your spending. It's the only way to make sure that you are executing your plan properly and that your vision is becoming closer to reality.

I constantly get asked which budgeting app is the best. My answer is always the same: it depends. We all process information differently, prefer different formats for information, or want different levels of involvement in the process. No one app is universally superior. I have friends who swear that Dave Ramsey's is the best, and other friends who hate it. Others love the YNAB app; but it, too, has detractors. Search the internet for recommendations, then just start trying out apps until you find one that works for you. Remember that this process is all deeply personal. Find a tool that works for you, no matter how long it takes!

2. REGULARLY COMPARE ACTUAL SPENDING TO YOUR PLAN

At the end of each month, compare your actual spending against your spending plan. Be sure to identify areas where you've overspent or underspent. Understand why each variance occurred. Was it a necessary adjustment, or was it due to impulse buying? Did you remember to refer to your spending strategy when you were considering these off-plan expenses? This thoughtful engagement of the process that led to these variances can give you greater insight into your own psyche's strengths and vulnerabilities.

3. REFLECT ON SPENDING HABITS

Monitoring your spending isn't just about keeping score. It's also about catching the small shifts before they lead you off course. One of the most valuable things you can do is pay attention to patterns, especially the ones that show up in places you didn't expect.

If you're consistently spending more than planned in a particular category, that's not just a math problem—it's a message. Ask yourself, *Why is this happening?* Are these impulse buys? Are you spending because you're tired, stressed, or emotionally drained after a long day? Are you using convenience to cope?

Maybe your grocery budget keeps getting blown because you're picking up takeout three nights a week. Not because you meant to, but because you're getting home late and you're exhausted. That kind of pattern doesn't just show you where the money's going. It reveals the friction between your plan and your reality.

And sometimes that friction isn't about self-control; it's about design. Your plan might simply be incomplete. Maybe you didn't budget enough for things that actually are important to you, like meals that save time, or gifts for friends, or self-care routines that help you stay grounded. That's not failure. That's feedback.

Your spending plan is a hypothesis. You start with what you *think* will work. Then life hands you more information. That's the process. Monitoring helps you learn what your real needs and rhythms are so you can refine your strategy over time. Adjusting your plan isn't backtracking. It's growing. It means you're paying attention.

This isn't about guilt. It's about clarity. When you notice your spending drifting off course, you're getting a chance to learn: *Is this a behavior I want to change, or a signal that my plan needs to evolve?* It's a win either way, because either way you're building a system that fits *you* more closely.

That's the heart of a good strategy. Not rigidity, but responsiveness. Not perfection, but progress.

Because once your habits shift, your future does too.

THE THOMPSONS' 80/20 SPENDING PLAN

Let's revisit the Thompson family.

The Thompsons' financial life is guided by three core values: family time, education, and security. Their goals reflect those values across different time horizons: paying off credit card debt and building their emergency fund in the short term, saving for their children's enrichment and a reliable family vehicle in the medium term, and funding college, an early mortgage payoff, and retirement in the long term.

To bring those goals to life, they developed a spending strategy that prioritizes what matters most while keeping day-to-day choices simple and sustainable. Their approach is rooted in clarity: They pre-decided which types of spending align with their values, which ones deserve limits, and which should be avoided. That strategy gave them the structure to build an 80/20 spending plan—allocating the first 20 percent of their income to financial goals and using the remaining 80 percent for all other expenses. This way, they ensure their most important priorities get funded first, but they still enjoy flexibility and joy in their daily lives.

MONTHLY NET INCOME: $8,000 (ASSUMED AFTER TAX FOR SIMPLICITY)

Twenty Percent to Financial Goals ($1,600/month)

This portion is nonnegotiable. It's the first thing funded every month, before bills, fun, or extras.

- Retirement Contributions: $1,000/month automatic transfers to IRAs and 401(k)s to stay on pace for their $1.5M goal

- College Savings + Enrichment: $250/month dedicated to kids' educational costs, camps, and extracurriculars

- Emergency Fund Growth or Credit Card Payoff: $350/month; until the $5,000 credit card is paid off, this fund can accelerate repayment—afterward, it shifts toward rebuilding or growing their emergency fund

Eighty Percent for Living Expenses and Enjoyment ($6,400/month)

This covers everything else: housing, transportation, food, insurance, lifestyle spending, and entertainment.

- **Essentials** (approx. $4,500/month): mortgage and utilities, groceries and household needs, insurance (health, home, auto), car loan payment, childcare/school-related costs

  ◦ **Lifestyle & Value-Aligned Spending** (approx. $1,200/ month): weekly family breakfasts and monthly outings; books museum passes, educational apps; preventive health/home maintenance

  ° **Discretionary & Flex Spending** (approx. $700/month): dining out twice a month; fun money for each adult; subscriptions; small impulse buys, gifts, and unexpected wants

WHY IT WORKS

By locking in their 20 percent for financial goals *first*, the Thompsons ensure they're always making progress no matter how the rest of the month plays out. The remaining 80 percent gives them flexibility, comfort, and the ability to enjoy life in a way that still aligns with their values. It's disciplined but livable—a plan that moves them forward without feeling like a grind.

START SMALL

If you're looking at your budget and thinking, *There's no way I can set aside 20 percent for savings or debt right now*, that's okay. You don't need to hit the perfect number to get started—you just need to *start*.

Set aside $10. That's it. If you can manage $50, even better. The amount doesn't matter nearly as much as the habit. Because what you're really building isn't just a savings balance—it's a mindset. A habit of directing your dollars with intention. A system that puts you in charge. Those early steps may feel small, but they're powerful. They create momentum.

And that momentum compounds.

There's a kind of quiet thrill in watching your accounts grow—$10 to $100, $100 to $1,000, $1,000 to $5,000. You start to feel not just more secure but also more confident. More capable. More in control. No impulse buy can compete with that.

You don't need the perfect moment or the perfect plan. You need action. You need alignment. You need to start with what you've got and let your habits do the heavy lifting from there.

MOMENTS OF CLARITY

- **Your spending plan is where strategy meets reality.** It's how you turn goals into action, paycheck by paycheck.

- **There's no "right" budget**—just the right one for you. Choose a structure that fits your life and adjust it as needed.

- **Spending without monitoring leads to drift.** Track your patterns to catch misalignment early and course-correct with purpose.

- **Plans should evolve with your life.** If your spending keeps clashing with your plan, it might be time to update the plan, not just your behavior.

- **Start small.** Stay consistent. Even $10 a month builds the habit. Habits build momentum. And momentum builds wealth.

CHAPTER ELEVEN

CREATE YOUR FINANCIAL PLAN

I n the previous chapter, we saw how the fictional Thompson family created a spending strategy rooted in their values and goals, and how that strategy shaped the way they use money every day. Now it's time to build your own.

This chapter gives you a set of simple, flexible templates to help you design a financial plan that reflects your life, your values, and your goals. These aren't fill-in-the-blank budget worksheets. They're tools to help you think clearly and act intentionally—starting with the big picture and working down to practical details.

You'll find templates to help you clarify your financial vision (your *why*), articulate your spending strategy (your *how*), and map out spending plans (your *what*) for different timeframes. Whether you're building a monthly plan, tracking toward a long-term goal, or simply trying to spend with more purpose, these frameworks will help you stay aligned and in control.

Think of this chapter as your planning toolkit. Use what fits, adapt what doesn't, and return to it anytime you need to recenter or make a change. You don't need a perfect plan—you just need a plan that keeps pointing you in the right direction.

TEMPLATE—CREATE YOUR FINANCIAL VISION

Answer the questions in this template to start creating your own vision for your life. If you feel unsure about certain parts, skip them. You can revisit them later once you've had more of a chance to consider them.

STEP 1: PERSONAL VALUES AND PRIORITIES

- Core Values: What matters most in your life? (e.g., family, health, community, personal growth)

- Top Priorities: What are your current focuses? (e.g., spending more time with loved ones, improving health, advancing in your career)

- Happiness-Spending Insights:
    - What purchases bring lasting happiness and satisfaction? (e.g., meaningful experiences, hobbies)
    - What purchases do you regret or find unnecessary?

STEP 2: PERSONAL LIFE GOALS

- Short-Term Goals (1–2 years): What do you want to accomplish soon? (e.g., develop a skill, create family traditions, organize your home)

- Intermediate Goals (3–5 years): What are your medium-term aspirations? (e.g., deepen community involvement, strengthen relationships, pursue hobbies)

- Long-Term Goals (5+ years): What is your vision for the future? (e.g., maintain strong family ties, mentor others, travel, achieve personal growth)

STEP 3: FINANCIAL REQUIREMENTS

- Estimated Costs: What are the approximate dollar amounts needed to support your goals?

- Savings Targets: How much do you need to save monthly or annually for each goal?

- Goal Prioritization: Rank your goals based on importance and available resources.

STEP 4: SPENDING WEAKNESSES AND CONTINGENCY PLANS

- Spending Weaknesses: Where are you likely to overspend? (e.g., impulse buys, lifestyle inflation)

- Contingency Plans: What strategies can you use to stay on track? (e.g., "fun money" budget, automatic savings, purchase delays)

TEMPLATE—CREATE YOUR SPENDING STRATEGY

Use this template to create your personalized spending strategy. Reflect on your values, priorities, and spending patterns to align your financial decisions with your long-term vision.

STEP 1: TOP PRIORITIES

"I will ensure that I . . .":

List the most important financial and personal goals that you want to prioritize. These are the areas where you want to allocate your money first.

Examples: Save for retirement, fund family experiences, or invest in education.

1. _____

2. _____

STEP 2: LIMITED SPENDING AREAS

"I will limit spending on . . .":

Identify areas where you want to spend cautiously. These are still important, but not as critical as your top priorities.

Examples: Dining out, entertainment, or clothing.

1. _____

2. _____

STEP 3: SACRIFICES

"I will sacrifice . . .":

List the expenses you plan to cut back on or eliminate entirely in order to focus on what matters most.

Examples: Delivery services, impulse purchases, or premium subscriptions.

1. _____

2. _____

STEP 4: PLAN FOR CASH RESERVES

Develop your priorities for building, maintaining, and using your cash reserve by answering the following questions:

1. How much cash would you like to have on hand in a savings account for emergencies?

    o _____

2. How will you build up that amount of money?

    o _____

3. Are you willing to dip into that reserve to pay for discretionary expenses, like cars or trips? If so, to what point are you willing to draw down your reserves?

    o _____

STEP 5: SPENDING WEAKNESSES AND GUARDRAILS

WEAKNESSES:

Identify the areas where you tend to overspend or struggle to control spending.

1. _____
2. _____

GUARDRAILS:

Plan strategies to help you avoid overspending in these areas.

1. _____
2. _____

KEY PRINCIPLES FOR YOUR SPENDING STRATEGY

- Prioritize spending on areas that bring long-term happiness and align with your vision.

- Minimize or eliminate trivial or impulsive expenses that don't add real value.

- Prepare for unexpected challenges by identifying flexible areas in your budget.

This guide will act as your financial compass, helping you stay focused on what matters most while giving you control and clarity over your spending.

TEMPLATE—CREATE YOUR OWN SPENDING PLAN

You can find templates to help you create a spending plan that fits your style at: strategicmoneymethod.com/tools. We offer options for all three types of plans discussed here (fixed-expense focused, savings focused, and every-dollar focused).

MOMENTS OF CLARITY

- **Start with your *why*:** Clarify your core values and life goals before diving into numbers. Your financial plan should reflect what matters most to you.

- **Use flexible templates, not rigid budgets:** The tools in this chapter are designed to help you think clearly and act intentionally, not force you into a one-size-fits-all budget.

- **You don't need a perfect plan—just a functional one:** Focus on progress and alignment, not perfection. A plan that keeps you pointed in the right direction is enough.

- **Templates available:** Download all three plan styles— fixed expense, savings focused, and every dollar—at strategicmoneymethod.com/tools.

PART 3

INTENTIONAL BORROWING

CHAPTER TWELVE

THE "SECRET" SUPERPOWER OF DEBT

My friend Rachel prided herself on being debt-free for life. No credit cards. No loans. No financing, ever. If she couldn't pay cash, she didn't buy it—end of story. On paper, it sounded admirable. But in real life? It was a different story.

Rachel once spent three years saving up to buy a used car—in the meantime driving a barely functioning clunker that broke down twice a month and cost her a fortune in repairs. She refused to take out a modest auto loan, even though she had good credit and stable income. "I'm not going into debt for a car," she told me. "That's how they get you."

The irony was that in the long run, her refusal to borrow actually cost her more. Missed work. High repair bills. Towing fees. And the stress.

She was free from debt, but not from financial stress. Her determination to avoid borrowing made her life harder, not easier.

Rachel is not alone. A lot of people treat debt the same way. To them, the best way to handle debt is simple: never touch it. Avoid it like it's radioactive. Pay cash for everything. If you don't owe anyone anything, you can't get in trouble, right?

That mindset is understandable. It's rooted in caution and a desire to stay in control. And for some people, especially those recovering from past financial mistakes, a debt-free approach might be exactly what is needed. But for others, swearing off all debt is a bit like using a hammer to fix your glitchy computer. It might feel satisfying, but it doesn't actually solve the problem—and it can do more harm than good.

Debt, at its core, is just a tool. And refusing to use a tool out of fear doesn't make you safer, it just limits what you can build. A well-structured loan can create access, mobility, and opportunity. A carefully managed mortgage can help you grow wealth. Even strategic credit card use, when done wisely, can provide convenience and rewards.

Intentional spending is the cornerstone of any solid financial plan. It helps you align your spending with your values, track your progress toward goals, and maintain a sense of control over your money. But as life evolves, you'll likely encounter situations where budgeting alone won't get you everything you need or want. That's where debt can prove its value.

At its core, debt allows you to buy time. It lets you acquire something today and pay for it over time, often with interest. For many of life's larger expenses—such as buying a home, financing higher education, or starting a business—debt is not just useful but often necessary. When managed properly, debt can help you build wealth, create opportunities, and achieve dreams that might otherwise feel out of reach.

However, debt is not without risks. The key to successfully using debt lies in three key considerations: focusing on the function debt serves, weighing the costs and benefits of borrowing, and evaluating alternatives. These principles ensure that any debt you take on aligns with your financial vision and long-term goals. With a clear strategy, you can ensure debt works as a tool that empowers you to achieve your financial goals rather than a burden that hinders progress.

DEBT BUYS TIME

Debt is a tool—a powerful one that allows you to buy something far more valuable than money: time. And in the economy of life, time is the ultimate currency. You can earn more money. You can cut back on expenses. But you can't mint more hours in a day or add more years to your prime.

When I say debt buys time, I don't mean in some abstract, philosophical way. I mean it literally. A student loan can buy you time to pursue an education now, rather than spending a decade saving for tuition while putting your dreams on hold. A mortgage can let you start building equity and stability today, instead of spending years bouncing between rentals hoping housing prices don't outpace your savings. Even a business loan can give you the time to focus on growth and revenue instead of grinding out progress inch by inch with only what you can self-fund.

In each of these cases, debt lets you pull future possibilities into the present.

That's the real value of debt: the access, not the cash. It can open doors that might otherwise stay closed for years—maybe forever. It gives you time to live in the house while your kids are still young, or launch the business while the opportunity is hot, or invest in yourself while your motivation is highest. It's a way of saying, "I'm not waiting for permission to move forward—I'm starting now."

Kenneth was determined to buy a house without debt. No mortgage, no interest, no banks. Just cash. He figured if he lived frugally and saved aggressively, he could put together $250,000 in fifteen to twenty years. So he moved back in with his parents after college, drove an old car, skipped vacations, and funneled every extra dollar into savings.

By his early thirties, he had over $215,000 in the bank—an impressive feat. But housing prices had outpaced his progress. That $250,000 starter home he'd once had his eye on? Now it cost closer to $375,000. His savings had grown, but the goal had drifted further out of reach.

And while his bank account was healthy, the rest of his life felt stuck. Dating from his parents' basement was awkward. Marriage felt premature without a home or apartment to share. Kids? Not without space. Meanwhile, his friends who had taken out mortgages were building lives. Paying interest, yes. But also building equity, decorating nurseries, hosting dinners, making memories.

Kenneth had avoided debt, but he couldn't avoid time. And time had quietly taken what he couldn't get back: his twenties, his independence, the early chapters of the life he wanted.

Kenneth's story illustrates an essential principle: Our key isn't to focus on cost alone—it's to focus on both costs and benefits. Yes, a mortgage can be very expensive, but that's okay if it provides a correspondingly high benefit. In Kenneth's case, it could've bought ten to twenty years of living life the way he wanted. That's a pretty big benefit! This is why it's so important to be clear about the benefits of debt. And the primary benefit debt provides is time.

HOW MUCH ARE YOU WILLING TO PAY FOR TIME?

The question isn't whether debt is good or bad. It's about whether the time you're buying with debt is worth the cost. For example, taking on student loans to finance higher education might allow you to start your career years earlier, opening professional doors and gaining valuable experience that can greatly increase lifetime earnings. Similarly, financing a home through a mortgage can enable you to build equity and enjoy stability without waiting decades to save up enough to purchase it outright.

On the other hand, there are situations where it may not make sense to use debt. Borrowing money on a credit card for something like a pair of shoes or a video game may not provide enough value to justify the cost of borrowing. The benefit of buying time in these cases is minimal, and the debt may simply add financial strain without delivering significant advantages.

EXAMPLES OF TIME THAT DEBT CAN BUY

Let's look at specific examples of how much time debt can buy, complete with figures and calculations.

EXAMPLE 1: BUYING A HOME

Let's look at the numbers for Kenneth's situation. He wanted to purchase a home worth $250,000. Saving for this amount without debt might take twenty years if he could save $12,500 annually (a daunting task for most people). Alternatively, he could have taken out a thirty-year mortgage with a 6 percent interest rate. Assuming a 20 percent down payment ($50,000), his loan amount would be $200,000. Here's what this looks like:

Scenario	Time to Ownership	Monthly Payment	Total Cost (Principal + Interest)
Save and Buy	20 years	N/A	$250,000
Mortgage (6% APR)	Immediate	$1,199	$431,680

TABLE 12.1

We often approach borrowing with the wrong questions. Most people ask, "Can I afford the $1,199 monthly payment?," which ignores all cost and benefits. Others dig deeper and ask, "Do I really want to pay $181,680 in interest for a $250,000 home?" which does consider cost but ignores benefit.

But both miss the deeper point. The better first question to ask is: "Is twenty years of comfort, stability, and independence worth the $181,680 in added cost?" Debt isn't just about math—it's about what that borrowed money makes possible. When you reframe the question around the *value* of the time you're buying with interest, you get a much clearer picture of whether the trade-off is worth it.

EXAMPLE 2: BUYING A CAR

Suppose you need reliable transportation and are considering a car priced at $25,000. Saving for the car might take you four years at $500 per month, but an auto loan at 8 percent interest for five years would allow you to buy the car immediately.

Scenario	Time to Ownership	Monthly Payment	Total Cost (Principal + Interest)
Save and Buy	4 years	N/A	$25,000
Auto Loan (8% APR)	Immediate	$507	$30,414

TABLE 12.2

We tend to focus on the $5,414 in interest and ask, "Do I really want to pay more than the car is worth?" But the better question is: "Is four years of reliable transportation, flexibility, and opportunity worth $5,414?" A car loan doesn't just buy a vehicle—it buys time, mobility, and access. If having the car now lets you get to a better job, avoid costly breakdowns, or simply live with less daily stress, that added cost might be a bargain, not a burden.

EXAMPLE 3: FINANCING A NEW WATER HEATER

Now consider a smaller but urgent purchase: replacing a broken water heater that costs $4,000. You adjust your spending plan so you can pay about $500 per month towards it. Without savings, you might put the expense on a credit card with a 20 percent interest rate, planning to pay it off over eight months.

Scenario	Time to Replacement	Monthly Payment	Total Cost (Principal + Interest)
Save and Replace	8 months	$500	$4,000
Credit Card (20% APR)	Immediate	$500	$4,328

TABLE 12.3

When faced with a $328 interest charge on a credit card, it's easy to think, *Why pay more than I have to?* But the better question is: "Is eight months of hot water worth $328?" In situations like this, borrowing isn't about luxury, it's about necessity. A working water heater means showers, clean dishes, and basic comfort. If the alternative is going without hot water for weeks or months while you save, the cost of interest may be a small price to pay for restoring normalcy right away.

Don't get the wrong idea—every time you use debt, you're trading away a bit of future wealth. I'm not advocating that you borrow as much as possible just because sometimes it's worth it. The goal is to rethink how you approach borrowing decisions. Over time you should be building a solid financial base: an emergency fund, positive monthly cash flow, and short-term savings for the everyday curveballs life throws at you, so you're not relying on debt for every bump in the road. But when time matters and paying cash isn't an option, debt doesn't have to be destructive. Stay focused on what debt can buy—*time*—and use it intentionally. That's how borrowing becomes a tool for progress instead of a drain on your future.

DOES THE DEBT ALIGN WITH YOUR GOALS?

Understanding how much time debt provides is critical to determining whether it's useful or harmful. If the debt allows you to gain significant time and that time is highly valuable, it may make sense to take on the expense.

However, if the time gained is negligible or the benefits are not substantial, the debt may not be worth it. Recognizing this balance between cost and benefit is the first step in using debt wisely. For example, consider Jenna. As part of a class assignment, she wrote about a time she fell in love with a $500 pair of designer shoes. They were elegant, made her feel confident, and seemed perfect for a few upcoming events. She didn't want to wait, so she put them on her credit card. Thanks to interest, by the time she finished paying them off over the next year, she had spent about $560 on them.

If Jenna had saved for just four months, she could've bought them with cash. So in effect, she paid an extra $60 to have them four months sooner. That's about 50 cents per day for four months. But here's the thing—she didn't wear them every day during those four months. She wore them just three times. So that $60 didn't buy her four months of daily joy. It bought her three early wears. That's about $20 per wear, just because she paid on a credit card.

There's nothing wrong with treating yourself, and Jenna doesn't regret the shoes overall. However, once she did the assignment and calculated how much she had paid for the time, she concluded that perhaps that hadn't been a very efficient use of debt.

Applying a value to something as intangible as time is challenging, and the value of a certain amount of time will vary from person to person and from purchase to purchase. What feels like a worthwhile investment of time for one individual may not hold the same value for another. As in everything, the key is to stop and think. Carefully identify exactly how much time you are buying with debt and assess whether that time aligns with your priorities and goals.

It's easy to focus solely on the price tag of debt and view it as a burden, but doing so misses the point. Debt is a tool for achieving your financial vision and aligning your spending with your values. By focusing on the benefits—particularly the time it provides—you can make intentional decisions about when and how to use debt. Remember, expensive debt can still be valuable if the time it buys is meaningful and aligned with your goals.

In the next chapter, we'll dive deeper into the costs associated with debt and learn how to evaluate those costs and determine whether they're justified by the benefits. For now, keep in mind that debt, when used intentionally, can be a powerful tool to help you live the life you want sooner and for longer.

MOMENTS OF CLARITY

- **Debt is a tool, not a trap.** When used intentionally, debt can help you access opportunities, stability, and independence that would otherwise take years to reach through saving alone.

- **The true value of debt is time.** Debt allows you to bring future possibilities into the present, whether that means a home, education, reliable transportation, or basic necessities.

- **Evaluate debt through the lens of your goals.** Ask how much time you're gaining, what that time enables you to do, and whether it fits your long-term vision, not just your short-term comfort.

CHAPTER THIRTEEN

THE COSTS OF DEBT

There's a classic *Saturday Night Live* skit from 2006 that still makes me laugh—and wince—a little every time I watch it. Steve Martin and Amy Poehler play a couple thumbing through a catalog of temptations: boats, flat-screen TVs, designer furniture, etc. Chris Parnell, playing a financial guru, introduces them to his revolutionary new program for managing debt called Don't Buy Stuff You Cannot Afford. The skit went something like this:

"But what if we *want* something and don't have the money?" they ask.

"You *don't buy it*," he explains.

"But what if it's on sale?"

"You *still* don't buy it."

"Sounds confusing."

The couple stares at him, baffled.

It's hilarious because it's so blunt and relatable. But it also hits a nerve for me as a financial professional and educator—because the real world doesn't operate like that.

In real life, "Can I afford it?" is a much slipperier question than it seems. The challenging reality is that how you pay for something affects how much it costs, which in turn affects whether or not you can "afford it." It's not just about whether you have the money today; it's about how you plan to pay, and what the consequences of that plan are. Paying cash, putting it on a credit card, financing it over five years—depending on which option you choose, a purchase of the exact same item can have very different financial costs and outcomes. Loans have the power to reshape the price, stretch your budget, and compound the impact of your choices.

When using debt to make a purchase, it's essential to separate the cost of the item being purchased from the cost of the loan itself. The aggregate costs of the loan are known as *finance charges*, and these charges come in various forms. While interest is the best-known finance charge, it's not the only one—and it's not even always bad.

UNDERSTANDING FINANCE CHARGES

Finance charges, including interest, are the cost of using a loan. Whether these charges are "good" or "bad" depends entirely on the value of the time you're receiving in return. For example, it may be worth it to pay interest on a mortgage that allows you to enjoy a home decades sooner than you otherwise would. Conversely, high-interest credit card debt for a discretionary purchase like a video game may not be.

Financing charges come in many forms. Interest is the best known, but there are also origination fees, service charges, penalties, and even terms that make repayment more expensive over time. These costs can add up quickly, and when they're lumped together with the price of the item, it's easy to lose track of what you're really paying for.

That's why keeping the item's price and the loan's cost separate is so important. It forces you to ask clearer questions: *How much extra am I paying for the privilege of time? Is it worth it?* Sometimes it is. But you can't answer that until you see both parts of the equation: the cost and the benefit.

Many financing charges are charged up-front. These include origination fees, application fees, or closing costs on loans. It's crucial to read your loan paperwork carefully to understand these charges. Finding less expensive loans is part of Key Question number three, which asks, *Is there a smart swap?* Not only can you shop for an alternative to the item itself, but you can shop for less expensive loan options as well. For example, our truck-loving friend Trevor can consider alternatives to the truck itself, but he can also explore whether his credit union will give him a less expensive loan than the one offered by the dealership.

SHOPPING FOR THE BEST LOAN TERMS

Debt can be a strange thing. Common sense tells us that the thing with the lower price is the less expensive option, but that's not always true with debt. The loan with the lowest monthly payment (and therefore the most "affordable") isn't necessarily the least expensive option in the long run. In fact, in many cases the loan with the smallest payment will be the *most* expensive, not the least. This makes debt tricky to evaluate, because low payments often come with extended loan terms that significantly increase the total cost. While it can get more complicated, there are several key factors that determine how expensive a loan will be:

- Interest Rate: The percentage of the loan amount charged annually by the lender. A lower interest rate reduces the overall cost of borrowing.

- Loan Term: The duration of the loan. Longer terms mean lower monthly payments but higher overall interest costs.

- Up-Front Charges: Origination fees, closing costs, or other fees added at the start of the loan. These charges can significantly increase the cost of borrowing.

- Prepayment Penalties: Fees charged if you pay off a loan early. These penalties can negate the savings from paying less interest.

- Compounding Interest: For some loans, interest compounds frequently, adding to the cost. Understanding how often interest compounds is critical to evaluating a loan's true cost. You can see how often a loan compounds by reading the documents. It might not say "compound," but you can find the compounding frequency by looking for a section that talks about when interest is charged. Every time interest is charged, interest is compounded. I recommend avoiding loans that charge interest more frequently than once per month.

EXAMPLE: TWO LOANS FOR THE SAME PURCHASE

Suppose you're financing a $25,000 car and comparing two loan options:

Loan Option	Interest Rate	Loan Term	Monthly Payment	Cost of Car	Cost of Loan
Option 1	5%	5 years	$471	$25,000	$3,260
Option 2	4%	7 years	$341	$25,000	$3,644

TABLE 13.1

At first glance, Option 2 appears more affordable due to the lower monthly payment. However, the total cost of the loan is nearly the same due to the extended loan term. Additionally, Option 1 would allow you to pay off the debt faster, freeing up cash flow for other priorities sooner.

CHOOSE YOUR ONLINE CALCULATOR CAREFULLY

Online calculators can make loan calculations like these easy by allowing you to input the loan details and instantly see the costs. However, it's important to be cautious, because many online calculators are subtly biased to encourage you to choose the product they are selling. You can use the fair, unbiased calculators on my website for free!

EXAMPLE: CHOOSING BETWEEN FINANCING OFFERS

Let's consider Trevor, who has weighed his alternatives and decided to buy a new Ford F-150. He has negotiated a sales price of $35,000 and has a $5,000 down payment.

The dealership is offering 0 percent financing or an $8,000 discount if he chooses to finance through his bank. This is a common sales option for dealerships—you may have seen commercials saying, *Get zero percent financing or five thousand dollars same as cash at your local X dealership!* Sometimes they offer the discount as a refund after purchase (they usually call it "cash back" on commercials), and sometimes they offer it as a discount on the price (usually called "same as cash" or "total savings" in ads) or something else similar.

In Trevor's case, they are offering a 0 percent interest loan if he gets his loan from the dealership (the phrase they use is "dealer financing" to indicate getting a loan from the dealership). If he chooses not to use the dealership's loan, then they will give him an $8,000 discount on the sales price, but he'll have to find a loan somewhere else.

Before reading this book, Trevor might have seen 0 percent and thought, *I know interest is bad, so I will choose zero percent. It's a no-brainer!* Fortunately, Trevor *did* read this book, and now he knows he needs to step back and consider his alternatives. He goes to his credit union and asks them for a quote on an auto loan for the truck. His credit union pre-approved him for a five-year car loan at 8 percent interest.

Trevor's efforts to pause and search out alternative loan options have presented him with a choice. He goes online and uses a calculator to do the math. Here's how the numbers break down:

Financing Option	Sale Price	Amount Borrowed	Monthly Payment	Financing Charges	Total Cost
0% Dealership Loan	$35,000	$30,000	$500	$0.00	$35,000
8% Bank Loan	$27,000	$22,000	$446	$4,765	$31,765

TABLE 13.2

With the 0 percent dealership loan, Trevor borrows $30,000 and pays $500 per month until the balance is paid off. Since there's no interest, his financing charges are technically zero—but he's still paying the full $35,000 for the truck.

With the 8% bank loan, Trevor borrows only $22,000, thanks to the $8,000 discount and $5,000 down payment. His monthly payment is lower—$446 instead of $500—and although he does pay $4,765 in financing charges over the life of the loan, his total cost comes to just $31,765. That's $3,235 less than the 0 percent offer.

This example reveals a critical insight: Financing offers don't exist in a vacuum. You have to consider the whole deal, not just the interest rate. Trevor isn't really deciding between 0 and 8 percent. He's deciding between paying more for the truck with no interest, or less for the truck with some interest.

If Trevor hadn't separated the cost of the loan from the cost of the truck, he might have made the wrong call. The 0 percent interest rate sounds appealing, but by focusing only on the financing terms and ignoring the bigger picture, he could have ended up paying more without realizing it. By laying out both the loan and the purchase price side by side, he could clearly see that the interest on the bank loan was far less than the $8,000 he saved on the truck.

Had he jumped at the dealership's 0 percent offer without exploring alternatives, he would have unknowingly paid an extra $3,235. That's the danger of not doing the math—some losses don't feel like losses at all. They're invisible. You don't see the $3,235 leave your account, but you also never got to keep it. Separating the item's cost from the cost of the loan—the cost of time—is what allowed Trevor to make a smart, informed decision.

ADJUSTING FOR HIGHER INTEREST RATES

Maybe you're thinking I cheated and cherry-picked a scenario to make my point. Fair enough. Let's stress-test it. Let's look at a different example where the numbers aren't quite as lopsided, and see if the principle still holds up.

Suppose Trevor's bank could only offer him a loan at 12 percent interest, rather than 8 percent interest. The calculations change, and the decision might shift:

Financing Option	Sale Price	Loan Amount	Monthly Payment	Financing Charges	Total Cost
0% Dealership Loan	$35,000	$30,000	$500	$0	$35,000
12% Bank Loan	$27,000	$22,000	$489	$7,363	$34,363

TABLE 13.3

Even at the higher interest rate, the bank loan remains less expensive than the dealership's 0 percent financing due to the discounted sale price. However, the savings margin narrows, demonstrating how rising interest rates influence decision-making.

Now let's reset the credit union interest rate to 8 percent and adjust the savings offer to $3,000 instead of $8,000. Under these conditions, Trevor should reconsider the dealership's 0 percent financing:

Financing Option	Sale Price	Loan Amount	Monthly Payment	Financing Charges	Total Cost
0% Dealership Loan	$35,000	$30,000	$500	$0	$35,000
8% Bank Loan	$32,000	$27,000	$547	$5,848	$37,848

TABLE 13.4

With a smaller discount, the dealership's 0 percent financing becomes the better option, highlighting how up-front charges and discounts can drastically affect the total cost of a loan. It's not about which loan *looks* better, but which one actually costs less once everything is on the table.

This is exactly why it's worth taking the time to run the numbers. These decisions can be surprisingly tricky, and small details can make a big difference. It takes time and effort to consider the full picture, but that effort can pay off big. Sometimes the smartest money move isn't the most obvious one.

ADDITIONAL HIDDEN COSTS

Finally, it's crucial to understand that every use of credit reduces your future financial flexibility. By borrowing, you are effectively taking money from your future to pay for something today. Every dollar spent on debt today is a dollar unavailable for future needs or opportunities.

Using debt is easy—intentionally so. Marketers and lenders have streamlined the borrowing process to encourage more borrowing, because that's how they make money. But remember that no lender is your friend. Their goal isn't to make your life better; it's to maximize their profit, which comes at your expense. Just because a borrowing option is easy doesn't mean it's wise. In fact, lenders often push borrowers toward the options that are most profitable for the lenders—which usually means more expensive for you. Don't blindly accept their suggestions, and don't default to the easiest path. Take the time to evaluate your options carefully. It's worth the effort.

Debt is also habit-forming. It's all too easy to charge purchases to a credit card and forget about them until the bill arrives, by which point you might not even remember what you bought. This pattern can create a dangerous cycle of borrowing from your future self without considering the long-term consequences.

Using debt can be beneficial and powerful, but it's not something to use casually or habitually. Be strategic. Choose your moments to use debt wisely and ensure it aligns with your financial vision and goals. Beware of the trap of easy borrowing because that path often leads to financial strain and diminished future opportunities. Thoughtful and intentional borrowing can make all the difference between building financial stability and falling into a cycle of unmanageable debt.

MOMENTS OF CLARITY

- **How you pay affects how much you pay.** The method of payment—cash, credit, or financing—can dramatically change the total cost of a purchase. Debt reshapes both price and consequences.

- **Separate the cost of the item from the cost of the loan.** Financing charges are the price you pay for *time*, not the item itself. Keep them distinct so you can judge whether the time is worth the cost.

- **Financing charges go beyond interest.** Look for origination fees, service charges, compounding frequency, and prepayment penalties. These often-overlooked details add up.

- **Lower monthly payments can be more expensive overall.** A smaller monthly payment may feel affordable but often hides a longer loan term and higher total cost.

- **Shop for better loans, not just better prices.** Just like finding alternative products to meet your needs, compare loan offers. The right financing choice can save you thousands.

CHAPTER FOURTEEN

EVALUATING LARGE PURCHASES

"Just don't buy stuff you can't afford!" If only it were so easy. Especially when it comes to big purchases.

For major financial decisions, how much something actually costs depends a lot on how you pay for it. Different financing options can lead to dramatically different outcomes. To get the most value for your money, you need to slow down, explore your alternatives, and find the option that offers the greatest benefit for the lowest overall cost.

This isn't something you need to do for every coffee or pair of shoes—that's where your spending strategy comes in, helping you stay aligned with your values in day-to-day choices. Nobody has the time or energy for deep analysis and consideration of each and every little purchase. You'll burn out your rational rider trying to do that. Spend the time strategizing about spending priorities in advance so you don't have to make so many choices each and every day. That's the purpose of the spending strategy we discussed in part 2.

But when the stakes are higher, the payoff for pausing and doing the math can be huge. Large purchases deserve your full attention, because the difference between a good deal and a bad one can run into the thousands each year, and hundreds of thousands or even millions in the long run.

START BY CONSIDERING LESS EXPENSIVE OPTIONS

The first alternative to consider is whether there is a less expensive option that still meets your needs. To aid in this search, you can use tools like Google, AI platforms, or input from family and trusted friends. These resources can help you discover alternatives you might not have considered and provide valuable insights into pricing and quality.

However, be cautious of recommendations found on social media. While it can be helpful to see options being discussed, many influencers are paid to hold your attention and promote the products of their sponsors. This means their advice may be biased, colored by the influence of sponsorship agreements rather than your best interests. Before making a decision, always verify the information you find and consider its source.

For many items, like cars, appliances, or furniture, this is relatively easy to research. Online reviews, price comparisons, and in-store negotiations can often reveal significant savings. Shopping for bargains, negotiating prices, and finding less expensive alternatives should be your first steps when evaluating a large purchase.

For other purchases, such as houses or education, finding less expensive alternatives may be more challenging. For example, you might explore neighborhoods with lower property values or consider whether attending an in-state university or starting at a two-year college could offer comparable education at a lower cost. These decisions require careful thought, as the options you choose can have a long-term impact on your finances.

The reason this process is so valuable for large purchases is that the financial stakes are higher. A small percentage of savings on a $200,000 house or a $30,000 car can add up to thousands of dollars over time. Additionally, the way you finance these purchases—whether through loans, credit, or savings—can significantly impact their total cost.

DECIDING ON HOW TO FINANCE YOUR PURCHASE

Once you've found a good product at a good price, it's time to consider how you wish to finance the purchase. Remember that the primary purpose of borrowing is to gain more time with the thing you're buying. For example, a mortgage allows you to live in your home decades sooner, and a car loan provides immediate access to reliable transportation. If you don't need to borrow to get more time—such as when you have cash saved and ready to use—you can enjoy the best of all worlds: immediate access to the item without the burden of financing charges.

But spending cash on hand has an often-overlooked drawback: you lose the opportunity to earn interest on that money. Sometimes that opportunity cost is small. But sometimes, as we'll see in an upcoming example, it can be significant.

That's why some people choose to use debt strategically, even when they *could* pay cash. By financing a purchase at a low interest rate and keeping their money saved or invested at a higher rate, they can earn more interest on their investments than they paid on the loan. This approach is usually called *leveraging debt*. I've done this myself in situations where the math clearly showed it was worth it.

A lot of people really like doing this, and it can be a powerful way to build wealth. But be careful. This approach only works if the interest you're earning is consistently higher than what you're paying—and only if you understand the full picture. Fluctuating investment earnings, hidden loan costs, or incorrect assumptions can erase any potential gain. So while this can be a smart strategy in certain cases, it's not one to try casually. If you're confident in your numbers and the stability of your interest earnings, go for it. If you're unsure, skip it. You'll do just fine without it.

The process I've been describing here can get pretty complicated, and we've already walked through a few examples that highlight the big picture. Now it's time to zoom in and break it down step by step so you can see exactly how to turn this kind of thinking into clear, effective action.

EXAMPLE: EVALUATING A SCOOTER PURCHASE

Alejandra wants to buy a scooter, and she wants to approach the decision intentionally and efficiently. She currently has $200 per month in disposable income, $500 in savings, $25,000 in her retirement account, and $7,500 in home equity. Here's how she might approach this decision:

STEP 1: RESEARCH ALTERNATIVE PRODUCTS

Alejandra first needs to find the right scooter for the right price. After doing extensive research, she discards a $1,200 scooter and a $13,000 scooter, and settles on one priced in the middle—$5,000. She feels this one provides the right performance without a hefty price tag.

STEP 2: IDENTIFY FINANCING OPTIONS

Alejandra identifies several ways to pay for the scooter:

- Current Income: She could save her $200 per month in disposable income and add it to her $500 in savings. However, it would take approximately twenty-three months to save the full $5,000, even with a 1 percent interest rate on her savings. This wait is a significant intangible cost of paying cash, and she needs to consider that when making her decision.

- Home Equity: She could take out a home equity loan. She searches online for a bank that gives home equity loans and gets a quote. This option involves closing costs of $2,000 and interest of $476 over three years at a 5 percent rate, for a total finance charge of $2,476.

- Retirement Savings: Alejandra could withdraw money from her retirement account. Doing so would incur a 10 percent early-withdrawal penalty ($660) and $940 in taxes. Additionally, she would lose out on $97,000 in potential investment interest if she left the $6,600 in the account to compound over time. The total cost of this option is $98,600.

- Credit Card: She could use her credit card, which has an interest rate of 22 percent. Paying $100 per month toward the balance would result in $8,700 in interest, while paying $200 per month would reduce the interest to $1,800.

STEP 3: ESTIMATE TOTAL COSTS

Alejandra calculates the total cost of each option:

- Saving with Current Income: $5,000 and a twenty-three-month wait

- Home Equity Loan: $5,000 + $2,476 = $7,476

- Retirement Savings: $5,000 + $98,600 = $103,600

- Credit Card at $100/Month: $5,000 + $8,700 = $13,700

- Credit Card at $200/Month: $5,000 + $1,800 = $6,800

STEP 4: EVALUATE BENEFITS

Each option offers different benefits and trade-offs:

- Saving with current income avoids financing charges but delays the purchase.

- A home equity loan has moderate costs and allows immediate access to the scooter.

- Withdrawing from retirement savings incurs significant costs, including lost future interest she could have earned from her investments.

- Using a credit card provides easy and immediate access but comes with high costs unless repaid quickly.

STEP 5: DECIDE AND EXECUTE

Now that Alejandra has analyzed her options, her decision comes down to this question: How much is she willing to pay to have the scooter now? Her most affordable options are the home equity loan and the credit card with $200 monthly payments. Each would cost her around $2,000 in financing charges. If Alejandra is comfortable paying an additional $2,000 on top of the scooter's $5,000 price tag, she can choose one of these options. The credit card is technically less expensive overall than the home equity loan, but it relies heavily on whether she is disciplined enough to pay it down quickly.

Unlike the home equity loan, which requires fixed monthly payments, the credit card option will only cost this much if she makes the conscious choice every month to pay extra on her credit card. Alternatively, Alejandra can choose to wait and save. While this option isn't as enjoyable in the short term, it may save her thousands of dollars in financing charges. Paying $2,000 in interest—almost half the cost of the scooter itself—might not feel worth it to her. Waiting requires patience, but it can save her a lot of money.

The key takeaway is that identifying the benefit (in this case, two years of scooter ownership) and weighing the costs has made Alejandra's decision clearer. If she had impulsively charged the scooter to her credit card and made only the minimum payments, she would have ended up paying $13,700—nearly three times the scooter's price—without even realizing it.

That's right: this would have been an invisible $13,700 expense. No letter would arrive in her mailbox to warn her of the final cost. Twenty years from now, when she looks back and wonders where all her money went, this impulsive decision would be one of the culprits, and she wouldn't even know it.

This is what's truly intolerable to me: Not the financing charges themselves, but the habit of making impulsive, unconsidered decisions that accumulate over time and very quietly drain financial resources. Paying interest or financing charges isn't inherently bad. It's the lack of awareness and intentionality that wreaks havoc on financial security.

But isn't it just a few thousand dollars? What's the big deal?

The big deal is this: if Alejandra chose the $200-per-month credit card option over the $100-per-month minimum payment option, she would save $6,900 ($13,700 minus $6,800) over two years. If she deposited that $6,900 as a one-time investment in her retirement account and earned a 10 percent annual return on it, it could grow to $120,000 by the time she retires in thirty years.

SMALL INEFFICIENCIES COMPOUND

Now imagine this scenario repeated over a lifetime. Obviously, she is not going to buy a new scooter every two years, but her habit of not making intentional, calculated borrowing decisions is likely to lead her to make similarly inefficient choices on an ongoing basis. If Alejandra saved $3,450 annually (the difference between the $200 and $100 credit card options) for thirty years and earned a 10 percent annual return, she would amass $567,000 in retirement savings. If she avoided unnecessary financing charges entirely—saving $13,700 every two years and investing that amount at 10 percent—she could build a retirement account worth over $1.1 million.

The math is clear: A lifetime of thoughtful, deliberate financing decisions can transform your financial trajectory. By consistently identifying the function of a purchase, weighing the costs and benefits (even for medium-sized purchases), and considering alternatives for both the scooter and the method of paying for the scooter, you can achieve a level of financial security that might otherwise feel out of reach.

WHAT NOT TO DO: WITHDRAW FROM YOUR RETIREMENT ACCOUNT

Alejandra's friend suggested another option to fund the scooter: withdraw money from her retirement account. For a hot second, Alejandra was tempted. The money was there, invested and growing slowly. Why not? After all, this would let her avoid paying interest on a loan and everyone knows that paying interest on loans is bad.

However, because she is under fifty-nine-and-a-half years of age, she would end up paying a 10 percent penalty for withdrawing early, as well as paying taxes on the amount withdrawn. Even worse, she'd lose out on the compounding over the long term, which is exactly what retirement funds need to do. Earlier, we calculated that she would lose about $97,000 in potential interest that money would have earned if she had just left it in the account.

When presented this way, withdrawing money from her retirement account seems like a ridiculous option. Sacrificing $97,000 in earnings for a scooter? Who would do that?

The answer is, unfortunately, almost everyone.

We don't necessarily think of this decision in these terms. What we do instead is cash out our retirement accounts regularly. Since 2009, over 85 percent of workers who have access to a retirement plan at work participate in that plan. That means they have money saved in their retirement accounts earning interest for them, just like Alejandra does.

However, when we leave our job (which Americans do every two to three years on average), we get a letter from the retirement plan provider. The letter says that we have money in our account, and if we want, they will send us a check for the balance. We read the letter and think *I could sure use $12,000!* (I mean, who couldn't?) So we check the box and have them send us the money.

This withdrawal costs us all the future interest that could have been earned.

Ouch.

MORE EXAMPLES OF HOW TO EVALUATE LARGE PURCHASES

Let's look at a few more examples of this process in action—buying a car, financing a home renovation, and planning a family vacation—to illustrate the process.

EXAMPLE 1: BUYING A CAR

Scenario: Tiana needs reliable transportation and is considering purchasing a car. She has her eye on a new sedan priced at $35,000. Tiana has $5,000 saved for a down payment, and she earns enough to afford up to $500 per month in car payments. She evaluates her options:

OPTION 1: FINANCING THROUGH THE DEALERSHIP

- Interest Rate: 0% APR
- Loan Term: 7 years
- Monthly Payment: $357
- Total Interest: $0 ($357 per month × 84 months – $30,000 loan amount)
- Total cost (car + interest): $35,000

OPTION 2: FINANCING A USED CAR

- Purchase price: $25,000
- Interest Rate: 5% APR
- Loan Term: 5 years
- Monthly Payment: $377
- Total Interest: $2,620 ($377 per month × 60 months – $20,000 loan amount)
- Total Cost (car + interest): $27,620

Analysis: The dealership's 0 percent financing makes the new car affordable with a lower monthly payment of $357 over seven years. However, the total cost remains higher than that of the used car, which would cost $27,620 after financing charges. The used car's higher interest rate increases the monthly payment to $377 but results in a shorter loan term of five years. Tiana must decide whether the benefits of a new car—such as a full warranty and potentially lower maintenance costs—justify the additional cost and extended loan term.

EXAMPLE 2: FINANCING A HOME RENOVATION

Scenario: Sophia wants to remodel her kitchen, and the estimated cost is $25,000. She has $10,000 in savings but will need to finance the remaining $15,000. She has considered her current spending and decides she can afford to set aside no more than $500 per month for this project. She uses online calculators to help her evaluate the following options:

OPTION 1: PERSONAL LOAN FROM HER BANK

- Interest Rate: 8% APR
- Loan Term: 3 years
- Monthly Payment: $470
- Total Interest: $1,920
- Total Cost (loan + savings): $26,920

OPTION 2: HOME EQUITY LINE OF CREDIT (HELOC)

- Interest Rate: 5% APR
- Loan Term: 5 years
- Monthly Payment: $283
- Total Interest: $1,980
- Total Cost (loan + savings): $26,980

OPTION 3: DELAYING THE PROJECT TO SAVE UP

- Monthly Contribution to Savings Account: $500
- Time to Save $15,000: 2.5 years
- Total Cost: $25,000

Analysis: Sophia's decision depends on how soon she wants to complete the renovation, and her tolerance for financing costs. The personal loan and HELOC have similar total costs, but the HELOC's lower monthly payment provides more flexibility. Delaying the project avoids financing charges but delays the benefits of the renovation. She needs to ask if it's worth waiting two and a half years to renovate the kitchen to save about $1,900.

EXAMPLE 3: PLANNING A FAMILY VACATION

Scenario: The Johnson family wants to take a dream vacation to Disney World, estimated to cost $8,000. They currently have $2,000 saved but would need to finance the remaining $6,000. They evaluate their options:

OPTION 1: CREDIT CARD

- Interest Rate: 20% APR
- Monthly Payment: $300
- Time to Pay Off: 24 months
- Total Cost: $7,200 in financing charges + $8,000 = $15,200

OPTION 2: PERSONAL LOAN

- Interest Rate: 10% APR

- Loan Term: 2 years

- Monthly Payment: $277

- Total Interest: $648 (calculated as $277 × 24 – $6,000)

- Total Cost: $8,000 + $6,648 = $14,648

OPTION 3: DELAYING THE TRIP TO SAVE

- Monthly Savings: $500

- Time to Save: 12 months

- Total Cost: $8,000 (no financing charges)

Analysis: Financing the vacation with a credit card would more than double the cost, making a credit card the least attractive option. A personal loan is more affordable, but delaying the trip to save avoids financing charges entirely. The Johnson family must weigh the benefits of enjoying the vacation now against the $6,648 savings from waiting.

PERKS OF HAVING SAVINGS

It's also important to note that having cash available in a savings account would allow Tiana, Sophia, or the Johnsons to make their purchases immediately without incurring any financing charges. For instance, in the case of the Johnson family's vacation, using $6,000 from their savings account would save them at least $6,600 in interest compared to financing the trip with a personal loan.

This highlights why building up cash reserves should be a high priority in any spending strategy. You can experience tremendous savings by avoiding the need to use debt for mid-sized expenses, whether they are emergencies or not. Additionally, having cash on hand provides the freedom to buy what you need when you need it, without jumping through lenders' hoops or incurring additional costs.

That said, it's equally important to replenish your cash reserves quickly after making a purchase. Maintaining a well-stocked savings account ensures you're always prepared for future expenses, enabling you to stay financially flexible and resilient.

MOMENTS OF CLARITY

- **The cost of a purchase depends on how you pay for it.** Financing choices can drastically change the real price you pay, sometimes adding thousands in hidden costs.

- **Use your spending strategy for small purchases; deep analysis is for big ones.** You don't overanalyze daily spending. Reserve your energy and attention for high-stakes decisions where the payoff for slowing down is high.

- **Identify *why* you're borrowing.** Debt buys you time—nothing more. Ask yourself how much you're willing to pay for earlier access.

- **Avoid impulsive decisions.** Quick purchases, especially with credit, can quietly cost tens of thousands over time. Without analysis, you won't even notice where the money went.

PART 4

EFFICIENT INVESTING

CHAPTER FIFTEEN

WELCOME TO THE WORLD OF INVESTING

When most people think about investing, they often imagine something loud and extreme. Maybe it's Leonardo DiCaprio in *The Wolf of Wall Street*, throwing cash and shouting into phones. Maybe it's the Reddit-fueled GameStop frenzy of 2021, with rocket emojis, meme stocks, and talk of "diamond hands." Or maybe it's TikTok influencers bragging about day trades and passive income while standing in front of rented Lamborghinis. Or maybe you're a bit old school and you think of the Gordon Gekko from 1987 movie *Wall Street* with his infamous slogan—"Greed is good"—and all the cutthroat energy that comes with it.

It's dramatic. It's intense. And it's . . . completely misleading.

These images, baked into our cultural consciousness, make investing seem like a high-stakes game only insiders or financial daredevils can play. No wonder so many people feel intimidated by it. They think if they don't have a finance degree or a high risk tolerance, they have no business investing at all.

But here's the truth: Investing doesn't have to be theatrical or complicated. In fact, for most people, the most effective approach to investing is remarkably boring. And boring is good. Boring means steady. Boring means repeatable. Boring means you don't have to watch the stock market like it's a bomb in a suspense thriller that's about to blow up.

It's important to demystify investing—not because you need to become an expert, but because you need just enough understanding to succeed. A little knowledge goes a long way. You don't need to predict the next market crash or find the next hot stock. You just need to understand a few key ideas, apply them consistently, and let time do the heavy lifting. No need to become Gordon Gekko or glue yourself to CNBC. Let's take investing off the big screen and bring it into your real life, where it belongs.

WHY INVEST?

Why park your hard-earned cash in an investment? Because it's the key to turning your financial goals into realities. Whether your goal is retirement, a child's education, or that dream vacation, investing can help you get there. It's about growing your wealth, outpacing inflation, and securing your financial future.

Let's look at an example. The chart below shows how much money you will have after thirty years if you start saving $500 today in different accounts. If you use a checking account that pays 1 percent interest, you will have about $209,000. If you use a high-yield savings account that pays 5 percent interest, you will have about $409,000—almost double!

But if you invest in the stock market the way I will teach you in this book and earn an average return of 12 percent per year, you will have a whopping $1.5 million.

That's right. The difference between just keeping your money in your bank checking account or investing it in the stock market wisely is over $1.3 million.

	Checking Account	High-Yield Savings	Stock Market
Monthly Savings	$500 per month	$500 per month	$500 per month
Number of Years	30 years	30 years	30 years
Interest Rate Earned	1%	5%	12%
Total Amount You Will Have Contributed	$180,000	$180,000	$180,000
Total at End of Investment	$209,838	$409,348	$1,540,486

TABLE 15.1. Behold the power of investing! Higher interest rates really add up over the years.

And that's why investing is important. Yes, it can be intimidating. Yes, it can feel scary. But the truth is that investing to earn interest and grow your wealth is essential for meeting long-term financial goals and becoming fully financially independent. And don't worry—it's not nearly as scary or intimidating as it might feel.

UNDERSTANDING RISK AND REWARD

At the heart of investing lies the concept of risk and reward. Risk is the chance that an investment's actual return will differ from the expected return, including the possibility of losing some or all of the original investment. Reward, or return, is the money you earn on your investments.

This relationship is fundamental. Generally, the higher the risk, the higher the potential reward. A savings account in a bank might offer low risk, but it also provides a meager return. Stocks, meanwhile, can swing high or low, offering the potential for greater rewards but also higher risks.

TYPES OF INVESTMENTS

Investments come in various forms, each with its own risk-reward profile:

1. **Stocks (Equities):** Buying a piece of a company. High potential returns, but also higher risk due to market swings.

2. **Bonds:** Lending money to a government or corporation. Generally safer than stocks, but with lower returns.

3. **Mutual Funds:** Pooling money with other investors to buy a diversified mix of stocks, bonds, and/or other securities. Offers automatic diversification, which can reduce risk.

4. **Exchange-Traded Funds (ETFs):** Similar to mutual funds but traded like stocks on an exchange. Offers diversification and lower fees.

5. **Real Estate:** Investing in physical buildings. Can provide rental income and capital appreciation but requires more capital and management.

6. **Certificates of Deposit (CDs), Money Market Funds, and Savings Accounts:** These are various types of bank accounts that hold your money but pay very little interest.

7. **Options, Futures, and Collectibles:** These are complicated and extremely risky investments. They are not suitable for amateur investors and should only be considered by those with advanced training and experience. The good news is that you absolutely do not need to use these to be a successful investor.

COMPARING LEVELS OF RISK

These investments can be best understood by placing them on the risk pyramid below. Investments at the bottom of the pyramid are relatively safe from losing money. For example, you don't have to worry about your savings account losing value because of the economy. On the other hand, stocks, real estate, and futures can produce lots of profit for you, but there's also a good chance you could lose money.

That's what I mean when I say there is a fundamental relationship between risk and reward. You can't make money without also taking on the risk of losing money. It just doesn't happen.

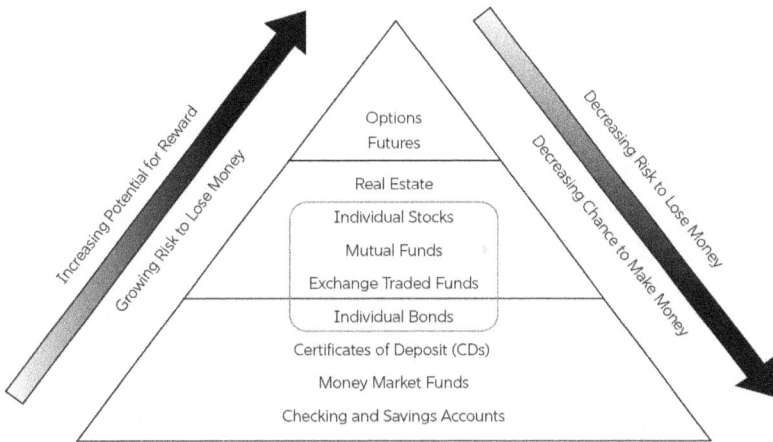

FIGURE 15.1. The Investment Pyramid—Risk vs. Reward.
You should ideally keep your investments within the center box.

That said, there is more than one risk in investing.

A lot of people think they're being "safe" by avoiding the market altogether—keeping all their money in a checking account or stashing it under the mattress. It feels secure because the balance doesn't go down. But here's the question: *Does it go up?*

Nope.

And that's the hidden threat. While it may seem like you're avoiding danger by not investing, you're actually embracing a different kind of risk: the risk of *stagnation*. These accounts at the bottom of the pyramid don't grow at any appreciable rate. They often don't even keep up with inflation over time. That means your money is slowly losing purchasing power, even if the number in your bank account stays the same or grows slightly.

If you're saving for retirement, a home, or future education costs, you don't need your money to just sit there. You need it to *grow*. And that only happens when you're willing to take on some level of investment risk in exchange for the potential of greater reward.

So yes, investing comes with risk. But so does *not* investing. Playing it safe can actually be one of the riskiest moves of all, because if your money doesn't grow, you will probably never reach the goals you're working so hard for.

Ideally, you should keep your investments in the middle of the investment pyramid: stocks, bonds, mutual funds, and ETFs. Other accounts are also helpful, but you don't use them as investments, because they are either too risky or they provide too little reward.

YOUR INVESTMENT GOALS AND TIME HORIZON

Your investment choices should align with your goals and the time you have to achieve them. Short-term goals, such as saving up for a vacation or a new water heater, might require safer investments from the bottom of the pyramid, while long-term goals, like retirement or saving for a child's college, can accommodate more risk for the possibility of higher returns.

INVESTING IS A JOURNEY, NOT A SPRINT

Remember, there's no one-size-fits-all in investing. It's about your goals, preferences, and time horizon. And you don't need a fortune to start. You're not trying to make a killing overnight; you're in this for the long run. Your job is to make consistent, informed decisions that accumulate wealth over time. The most effective investing strategy isn't flashy. It's methodical, consistent, and—let's be honest—a little boring. But that's exactly why it works. It stays focused on long-term growth, not short-term thrills.

But many investors get tripped up because boring doesn't *feel* like winning. They want excitement. They want action. And that hunger for something bigger, faster, and flashier often leads people to chase after the next big thing, whether it's a hot stock, a trending crypto, or the surefire strategy their cousin swears by on Instagram.

BORING IS GOOD

And patience pays off. Long-term investing isn't supposed to thrill you. If it feels like a roller coaster, you might be in the wrong seat. Steady, consistent, and a little boring? That's the ride that builds real wealth. Save the excitement for the amusement park.

Take, for example, a woman named Linda I met during a financial workshop. Back in the 1990s, she went all in on Beanie Babies. Not just collecting a few dolls as a fun hobby. *All in.* She genuinely believed it was a smart investment. She cleared out space in her home, spent thousands of dollars on limited editions, and followed Beanie Baby forums the way others follow stock tickers. At one point, her collection was valued at tens of thousands of dollars. Everyone around her said she was smart, ahead of the trend, even brilliant.

Until the Beanie Baby market collapsed. Practically overnight, the hype disappeared—and so did the resale value. What she thought was a clever investment turned out to be a textbook example of a speculative bubble: a surge in prices driven by excitement and hype instead of real value. She didn't lose money because she invested. She lost money because she *speculated*, chasing a hot trend instead of building long-term wealth the slow, steady way.

That's the trap: trying to be clever, getting caught up in hype, and straying from the fundamentals. In investing, getting fancy doesn't just distract you from your goal—it can steer you straight into a financial setback.

The good news is that you don't need to be a genius or have a dozen monitors lighting up your home office to get this right. You don't need to decode complicated charts or make trades at exactly the right second. You don't even need to check your investments every day. You just need a diversified portfolio, a clear plan, and the discipline to stick with it. The most powerful investment tool you have isn't a fancy algorithm or insider tip. It's time. So don't overthink it. Keep it simple, stay the course, and let your money do what it's designed to do: grow.

MOMENTS OF CLARITY

- **Boring is good.** The most effective investing strategies don't involve hype or high-stakes risks. They involve consistent, intentional decisions that quietly build wealth over time.

- **Use the middle of the pyramid.** Focus your investments in the sweet spot of the pyramid: stocks, bonds, mutual funds, and ETFs. Avoid investments that are too risky or too stagnant.

- **Investing is how money grows.** A checking account might feel safe, but it won't get you to retirement. Only investments that grow, like stocks, bonds, and funds, can build real wealth.

- **Your goals and time horizon matter.** The best investment depends on *what* you're saving for and *when* you'll need it. Short-term goals call for safer options. Long-term goals can accommodate more risk.

CHAPTER SIXTEEN

THE TROUBLE WITH INVESTING

I f you've ever watched *Back to the Future Part II*, you know the dream: take a sports almanac or a stock cheat sheet back in time, place a few bets or buy some shares, and return to the present as a billionaire. It's a classic fantasy. Hindsight investing. And it makes for a great movie plot.

In real life, though, we don't get almanacs from the future. It's easy to look back now and say, "If only I had bought Amazon in 2001." But at the time? Amazon was bleeding cash and still mainly sold books. Every market winner was once just another risky, uncertain bet.

The trouble with investing is that no one knows the future. No matter how compelling the story, how brilliant the founder, or how deep your research goes, there's just no crystal ball. Trying to pick the next big winner might make you feel smart, but it's often just a distraction from what really builds wealth.

Remember Microsoft in the early days? Okay, me neither. But just imagine it with me. Microsoft was just one tiny little company in Bill Gates's garage. It seemed to be run by a bunch of hippies and nerds, not top MBA graduates. This small group of people with little money and limited business experience was fighting against dozens of other companies that were also striving to bring personal computers into homes.

And Google? For a long time, Google was considered a latecomer—a fledgling search engine among a sea of competitors like Yahoo!, AltaVista, Dogpile, and Ask Jeeves—that had no chance of carving out a future in the internet search market. And yet, as we know, Google went on to become one of the largest and most influential companies in the entire world.

In both cases, predicting the overwhelming success of these companies over their competitors would have been akin to plucking a needle from a haystack . . . in the dark . . . during a windstorm.

THE ILLUSION OF FORESIGHT

When we look at companies like Microsoft and Google today, it's easy to think that *we* would've invested. Hindsight is tricky like that. But let's not forget that for every Microsoft, there are countless companies like Commodore or Netscape that also showed promise but ultimately couldn't keep up (RIP Dogpile, my old friend). The world of investing is filled with these stories—the almost-hits and near-successes. The stories of these companies are easy to forget as history leaves them behind, but they serve as a humbling reminder that not even the best businesses with the most innovative ideas are a surefire success.

It's tempting to treat a stock's past performance as a sign of future success. But the old saying holds: Past performance doesn't guarantee future results. If investing were as simple as chasing yesterday's winners, we'd all be rich by now. Unfortunately, markets aren't that generous—or that predictable.

A stock that's skyrocketed in recent years might just as easily crash in the next. Companies go through cycles. Industries shift. Consumer tastes evolve. Regulations change. Sometimes the very popularity of a stock can be its downfall, as prices get pushed far beyond what the business is actually worth.

Don't mistake momentum for a guarantee. A stock that went up yesterday might be due for a correction tomorrow. And by the time a stock's greatness is obvious, most of the gains are already priced in. Chasing past performance often leads investors to buy high and sell low—the exact opposite of what they should do to build long-term wealth.

FIGHT UNCERTAINTY WITH DIVERSIFICATION AND TIME

There are two powerful ways to deal with the uncertainty of investing. The first is diversification. That simply means spreading your money across different types of investments—stocks, bonds, real estate—as well as within those categories, like owning companies from different industries or countries.

Nick Fury gets this.

When the world was in danger, Nick Fury didn't just recruit Captain Marvel, he built an entire team: the Avengers. Sure, Captain Marvel is incredibly powerful—arguably the strongest hero in the Marvel universe. But even with all her strength, Fury knew better than to bet the fate of humanity on just one person. Instead, he assembled a team of heroes with different backgrounds, skills, and strengths. Iron Man brought tech and problem solving. Black Widow brought stealth. Thor brought raw power. Hulk? Unstoppable force. Captain America provided steady leadership and strategy.

Fury knew that no matter how strong one hero was, the team is what gave them the edge; no single superhero can do everything, especially when the threats keep changing. What works in one battle might fail in the next.

That's how diversification works in investing. You might have a favorite stock or asset—your Captain Marvel or Iron Man—but if you pour all your money into one place, you're vulnerable. Markets shift. Industries crash. Trends change. A diversified portfolio is like the Avengers: some investments provide growth, others provide stability, and some come through in emergencies. They balance each other out and protect you from the unexpected.

A diversified portfolio doesn't just help you survive tough times—it's often also the key to bouncing back faster. Like the Avengers helped bring the world back after Thanos's snap, your investment "team" gives you more tools to recover after a market crash. While one part of your portfolio may struggle, another may hold steady, or even thrive, and help carry you through. Diversification builds investment resilience.

You don't build a successful portfolio by picking one "super investment" and hoping it saves the day. You build it by assembling a smart, balanced, diversified team—one that can handle whatever comes next.

The other great weapon against uncertainty is time. Investing with a long-term perspective allows you to ride out the waves of market volatility. A long-time horizon can turn volatility from a threat into a tool. In the short term, markets can swing wildly on headlines, economic data, or investor emotion. But stretch your time horizon out to ten, twenty, or thirty years, and a remarkable pattern emerges: The longer you stay invested, the more predictable your returns become. In fact, over the long term the stock market has been *super* predictable. It can seem kind of weird and counterintuitive that something so chaotic and unpredictable in the short term can be so predictable in the long term, but it's actually a pretty common phenomenon.

Take me, for example. I am simultaneously chaotic and random as well as predictable. Here's how. When I ask myself, "What do I want for dinner next week?" the answer is "I don't know." On any given day, what I may be in the mood to eat is going to be largely unpredictable. I can't count how many times I've had a plan for dinner but pivoted last minute because a meal I usually like suddenly didn't sound that appealing. In the short run, my food preferences are random and unpredictable, just like the stock market.

However, over the long run, predictable patterns appear. I can't say for sure whether Arby's or Taco Bell will sound better next Tuesday, but if I look at my behavior in the past, I can make a prediction about the overall amount I will eat at these restaurants. If I look at my budget for the year and it shows I went to Arby's twice as much as I did Taco Bell last year, then I can conclude that I prefer Arby's over Taco Bell, but it does not mean that I will never go to Taco Bell. I can then reasonably predict that I will probably go to Arby's twice as often as Taco Bell in the coming year. Thus, the question of what I will be in the mood to eat next Tuesday is chaotic, random, and largely unpredictable, but my overall preference for Arby's over Taco Bell in the long run is highly stable and predictable.

These types of patterns aren't unique to investing and dinner. Weather is unpredictable day to day. You'd never try to guess the exact temperature next Tuesday or whether it'll rain three Thursdays from now. Daily weather is chaotic, shaped by shifting winds, evolving pressure systems, and unpredictable storms. But zoom out and it becomes surprisingly predictable. You know the summer will be hotter than the winter. You know the desert will stay drier than the rainforest. You don't need to predict every storm to pack the right clothes for the season.

The stock market is very much like that. Over the course of a few weeks or months, it's largely unpredictable. But over the course of five, ten, or twenty years, a different picture emerges. Suddenly the chaos gives way to steadiness. Over the long run, the market becomes surprisingly predictable, steadily rewarding patience and discipline. Just like you can't forecast Tuesday's rain three months from now, but you can count on summer being warmer than winter, you also can't predict next quarter's returns, but you can still be confident that staying invested over decades has historically led to growth.

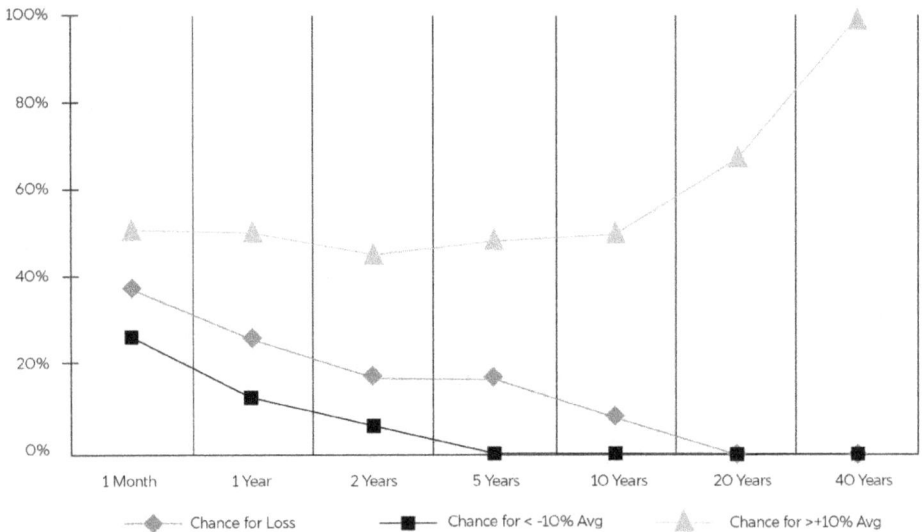

FIGURE 16.1. Performance of the stock market for various lengths of time. Note the far greater chance the market goes up (>10% average) leaves almost no chance for it to produce losses over the long term.

The chart above shows the returns of the stock market for the last seventy years for different lengths of time. The diamond on the left (in the "one month" column) means that the chance for loss over the course of one month is about 40 percent. That's high risk any way you look at it. However, by the time five years have passed, that chance is down to 20 percent, and after ten years the chance is 0 percent. That's right: zero. There has never been a ten-year (or longer) period of time where the stock market has produced a loss. None.

If we consider time periods with "significant performance" to be periods with more than 10 percent average loss or gain per year, we can see that if you were to have invested in the stock market for twenty years, you would have about a 70 percent chance of earning more than 10 percent per year. You only have a 50 percent chance for the same results over the course of one month. If you keep going and look at the forty-year column, you can see that there has never been a forty-year period in the history of the stock market that has failed to produce less than 10 percent returns per year.

This is what I mean when I say the stock market is quite reliable and predicable over the long run. You can't be sure exactly what your earnings will be. That's always true. But you can reliably trust that you are going to have consistently good returns; and that the longer you hold, the better your chances are of getting a great return.

But it's vital to note that *this rule applies only to the stock market as a whole*. Individual stocks, bonds, and mutual funds break this trend all the time. You will only get this long-term reliability if you purchase highly diversified investments. Don't worry, though, because diversified investing is super easy to do. I'll explain how in Chapter 17.

STAYING INFORMED, NOT OVERWHELMED

Staying informed is crucial, but there's a fine line between being informed and being overwhelmed. Constant news updates and market analysis can lead to overreaction. Remember, investing is not about reacting to every market movement but about sticking to a well-thought-out plan. In fact, research suggests that you will be a better investor if you just don't watch news about the stock market, because that news makes you emotional and emotion turns people into horrible investors![14]

Patience is not just a virtue in investing; it's a necessity. It's necessary to understand that while the market's movements can be erratic in the short term, your focus is on the long game. Rushed decisions often lead to mistakes. Patience fosters success.

EMBRACING THE UNCERTAINTY

Finally, embrace the uncertainty. Market ups and downs aren't bugs in the system. They're part of how investing works. Instead of fearing the next dip, plan for it. With a solid investment strategy, a well-diversified portfolio, and a long-term mindset, you can ride out the turbulence. When the market drops, don't panic—see it as a chance to buy great companies at a discount. And then? Stay the course. Investing isn't about timing the perfect moment; it's about staying in long enough to let time do the work. Keep your eyes on the horizon and hold tight, because you're in it for the long term.

---

14   Richard H. Thaler, Amos Tversky, Daniel Kahneman, and Alan Schwartz, "The Effect of Myopia and Loss Aversion on Risk Taking: An Experimental Test," *The Quarterly Journal of Economics* 112, no. 2 (1997): 647–661, https://doi.org/10.1162/003355397555226.

MOMENTS OF CLARITY

- **Diversification protects you from excess risk.** Rather than bet everything on one "super investment," build a team of different assets that can each thrive in different conditions. Diversification isn't flashy, but it's powerful.

- **Time transforms chaos into reliability.** In the short term, the market is unpredictable. But over decades, the chaos fades and trends emerge. The longer you stay invested, the more reliable your returns become.

- **Past performance is not a road map.** Just because a stock has done well doesn't mean it will keep doing well. Chasing past winners often leads to buying high and selling low—the exact opposite of what you want.

CHAPTER SEVENTEEN

HOW TO BUY LOW, SELL HIGH

W hen my brother-in-law was in middle school, he discovered a simple formula for making money: buy low, sell high. He'd go to the grocery store, pick up a twelve-pack of sodas on sale for a few bucks, then turn around and sell the individual cans at school for a dollar each. He made an impressive amount of money for a twelve-year-old and turned his locker into a vending machine.

Buy low, sell high—it sounds simple, doesn't it? It's the timeless law of making a profit and a staple of the investment industry. You buy a stock at a low price, then sell it later at a higher price to make a profit. Sounds so simple.

Yet in the unpredictable world of investing, timing the market perfectly to only buy when prices are low and only sell when prices are high is like trying to catch a falling knife. It's risky and, more often than not, leads to unpleasant outcomes.

That's why I love the dollar cost averaging strategy. There's no guess-work. No doomscrolling headlines. No 2:00 a.m. Google searches asking, "Should I sell everything?" This strategy just runs quietly in the background, doing its job while I live my life. I don't have to predict the market or be perfectly disciplined. I just have to stick with the plan. Set it once, let it do its thing—and watch my money grow.

UNDERSTANDING DOLLAR COST AVERAGING

Dollar cost averaging (or DCA) is an investment strategy where you invest a fixed amount of money at regular intervals—say, the 28th of every month, or whenever you get your paycheck—regardless of whether the market is up, down, or sideways. Think of it like setting cruise control on a long road trip. Instead of constantly speeding up, slowing down, or reacting to every curve in the road, you lock in a steady pace.

Cruise control doesn't just make long drives easier. It makes them safer too. You're less likely to get into an accident from sudden stops and starts, and you avoid getting speeding tickets from going too fast without realizing it. It reduces stress, saves fuel, and gets you where you want to go with less effort.

Dollar cost averaging works the same way in investing. It keeps you from overreacting to market volatility, stops you from chasing trends or trying to time the market, and helps you build wealth steadily over time. It's safer, simpler, and remarkably more effective—especially if you have a long road ahead.

And here's the magic: When prices are high, your fixed amount buys fewer shares. When prices are low, it buys more. Over time, that reduces the average amount you pay, because you automatically buy more cheap stocks and fewer expensive ones, making the average cost trend down. Dollar cost averaging gets its name from its remarkable ability to lower the average cost (in dollars) of the investments that you own.

HOW DCA WORKS

Let's say you decide to invest $100 into a mutual fund on the first day of every month. When the fund's price per share is low—say it's $50 a share on June 1st—your $100 buys two shares. When the price is high—say by July 1st it's up to $60 a share—that $100 buys less than it did a month earlier. Over time, this approach can lower the average cost per share you pay.

This effect is much more visible over a longer period of time. Table 17.1 shows the effects of using a DCA strategy to invest $100 at the beginning of each month over the course of twelve months, as the price of the stock fluctuated from $10 per share to $7 per share.

There are two important lessons to take away from this table.

First, take a look at the average price paid per share. Even though the stock was only below $9 for four out of twelve months, the average price paid over the year ended up being just $8.66 per share. That's the magic of dollar cost averaging. When the stock dropped to $7, the investor was able to buy more shares—over fourteen of them! That helped balance out the months when shares were more expensive, like when the stock hit $11 and they could only afford about nine shares. This balancing act lowers the average cost per share and sets the stage for better returns.

Second, look at the account value at the end of the year: $969.47. That's 15 percent higher than the $840 the investor would have had if they'd just invested the full $1,200 all at once in January. Why? Because in January, the stock was $10 per share, so $1,200 would've only bought 120 shares. By December, with the stock down to $7, those shares would've been worth just $840—a 30 percent loss. But with dollar cost averaging, the loss was much smaller—only about 19 percent. That's a huge difference!

HYPOTHETICAL EXAMPLE OF HOW DOLLAR COST AVERAGING WORKS OVER TWELVE MONTHS

Month	Price per Share ($)	Number of Shares Purchased	Total Shares Owned	Average Cost per Share ($)	Total Amount Invested ($)	Account Balance ($)
Jan	$10.00	10.00	10.00	$10.00	$100.00	$100.00
Feb	$9.00	11.11	21.11	$9.47	$200.00	$190.00
Mar	$8.00	12.50	33.61	$8.93	$300.00	$268.89
Apr	$7.00	14.29	47.90	$8.35	$400.00	$335.28
May	$8.00	12.50	60.40	$8.28	$500.00	$483.17
Jun	$9.00	11.11	71.51	$8.39	$600.00	$643.57
Jul	$10.00	10.00	81.51	$8.59	$700.00	$815.08
Aug	$11.00	9.09	90.60	$8.83	$800.00	$996.59
Sept	$10.00	10.00	100.60	$8.95	$900.00	$1,005.99
Oct	$9.00	11.11	111.71	$8.95	$1,000.00	$1,005.39
Nov	$8.00	12.50	124.21	$8.86	$1,100.00	$993.68
Dec	$7.00	14.29	138.50	$8.66	$1,200.00	$969.47

TABLE 17.1. Notice how the average amount paid per share declines over time because of fluctuations in the price. Source: Author calculations.

Not only was dollar cost averaging automatic, easy, and totally hands-off—it also turned out to be the smarter, more effective move.

Research has found that this is true even outside our small example.

THE BENEFITS OF DCA

- **Simplicity:** DCA takes the guesswork out of when to invest. It's a set-it-and-forget-it approach that doesn't require you to watch the market daily.

- **Reduced Impact of Volatility:** Spreading out your investments makes you less affected by short-term market fluctuations.

- **Discipline:** DCA encourages consistent investing, an essential habit for long-term financial growth.

IMPLEMENTING DCA INTO YOUR INVESTMENT PLAN

To start with DCA, determine how much you can comfortably invest regularly. Then choose your investment vehicle, be it stocks or mutual funds. Set up automatic deposits if possible, and then let the strategy work over time.

That's it.

THAT'S IT???

Yes, that's it. It's seriously that simple. Just let the automatic deposit do its job.

Once you set up automatic deposit, you have the easiest job in the world: do NOTHING. When the stock market goes up, what do you do? NOTHING. Just let the automatic deposit keep on going. When the market crashes, surely that's different? Nope. Your strategy is the same. Do NOTHING. Let your automatic deposits just keep on chugging along, smooth and steady. You will come out the winner in the long run.

LIMITATIONS OF DCA

While DCA is a sound strategy, it's not foolproof. It doesn't protect your account from going down in value. It doesn't give you the highest possible profits (that would require either a crystal ball, a Tardis, a DeLorean, or a hot tub time machine to show you the future). There will be times when you feel like you are making a mistake. Like it's stupid to keep investing when the market is crashing. It'll be scary. Oh boy, will it be scary. Investing during a crash is an incredibly scary thing.

But please trust the process. It has never failed in the entire history of the stock market. You will come out just fine, and in less time than you might think. For example, a person following this strategy in 2008 would have recovered all of their losses from the crash in just nine months' time! Someone who panicked and sold their investments often didn't recover their losses for at least five years.

No, DCA is not perfect, but it is remarkably effective and incredibly simple. Just keep on going. Set your monthly automatic deposit to your investment account and let it keep going. Just set it and forget it!

POWER OF DCA

DCA is not just simple and easy, it's also very powerful. By following DCA, you will get better investment results over the long term than if you sold all your stocks before a market crash and then didn't buy them back until after the market had recovered. The reason why this works is simple: a market crash means low stock prices, and low stock prices means that you can buy lots of stocks for very little money! When the prices inevitably rebound as the economy recovers, those cheap stocks you bought during the crash suddenly become very, *very* profitable.

I remember watching two of my neighbors go through the 2008 crash in very different ways. Let's call them Marcus and Ron.

At the time, I was a young finance grad—fresh out of school, full of book learning, and eager to see how real people handled real markets. I respected both of these men. Ron was sharp and confident, always reading up on market trends. Marcus was steady and practical, not one to get rattled. And as the financial world seemed to unravel around us, I watched closely, learning from how each of them responded.

When the market started tumbling, Ron sprang into action. "I saw it coming," he told me a hundred times. He pulled all his money out just before the worst of it hit. For months, he walked around with a quiet smugness, like he'd cracked the code. "I got out just in time," he confided to me one day at his house, nodding toward the flashing red numbers on the TV behind him.

Marcus did the opposite. As soon as the panic started, he turned off the news. Literally. He clicked off the TV, stopped checking stock reports, and just let his automated investments keep running. Every month, like clockwork, he just kept socking money away in his account. He didn't try to guess when the bottom would come. He didn't let fear make the decisions. He just tuned out the noise and stuck to the plan. The man was utterly unflappable.

At first it looked like Ron had won. The market was a mess, and Marcus's account balance kept shrinking. But then, almost as quickly as it had fallen, the market bounced back. Ron waited. He wanted to be sure it was safe. He didn't want to get back in too early. So he sat on the sidelines and watched. I was on the edge of my seat, watching to see if the theories my professors had taught me would hold out in the real world. Everything I knew from school at the time said Marcus would win, but my gut said Ron had the edge.

By the time Ron finally reinvested, the market had already climbed all the way back to where it was when he'd sold. "I didn't lose a penny! So much for this so-called Great Crash," he bragged. But while he was sitting in cash, Marcus had been buying cheap stocks the whole way down—and riding them all the way back up.

I created the chart below to tell Marcus and Ron's story after the fact. The black line is Marcus, steadily dollar cost averaging through the crash and the rebound. The gray line is Ron, who jumped out before the worst . . . but missed the best. (I know when Ron stopped investing, and when he started again, because he told me, but I had to infer Marcus's path based on his self-described DCA strategy.)

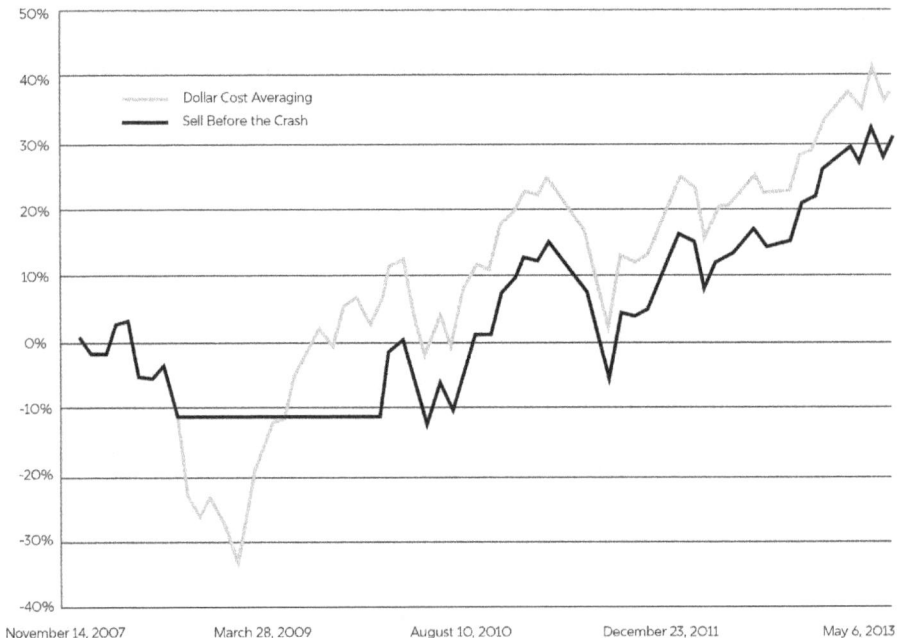

FIGURE 17.1. DCA vs. Selling before the Crash.
Marcus wins with dollar cost averaging!

Is there a winner? Did their strategies make a difference? The results are clear: yes, it made a difference. There's a clear winner, and it's not even close.

By the time the dust had settled, Marcus—who kept investing steadily through the crash—ended up with a portfolio 10 percent larger than Ron's.

That craziest part is that Ron didn't even do a bad job. In fact, his timing was fairly impressive. He got out before the worst of the crash and got back in early enough to catch part of the rebound. If we're being honest, that's better than most people manage. He should've been a textbook success story.

And yet he still lost to Marcus.

Why? Because while Ron was watching headlines, second-guessing himself, and trying to figure out the right time to jump back in, Marcus just kept investing. No drama. No stress. Just steady, automatic purchases at lower and lower prices. That's what made the difference.

Ron's timing was good. But what if it hadn't been? What if he'd waited a little longer? What if fear had kept him on the sidelines like it did for so many others? Many people never got back what they lost in the '08 crash; at least not for a long time. Some didn't reinvest for five years. Others waited a full decade. And in the meantime, the market left them behind.

Watching it all unfold, I had a realization that stuck with me.

My gut instinct—the part of me that wanted to believe I could time the market like Ron—had been dead wrong. And those "out-of-touch" professors I'd half-dismissed back in school? They had been right, and I had been naive. Dollar cost averaging wasn't just a theory from a text-book. It worked. It was simple, counterintuitive, dare I say boring . . . and completely brilliant.

Better results with less work and no guessing? Count me in!

A LONG-TERM STRATEGY

Doing nothing when the markets are crashing sounds simple—and it is. But it's not as easy as it seems. When you are watching your retirement savings fall day after day, you will experience fear, and that fear will push the primitive elephant in your brain to want to sell your stocks, get out of the market, and stop "losing" money. The fear of losing money is incredibly powerful. It can easily overwhelm even the most informed investors.

One of the most influential voices in my financial education was my doctoral professor and mentor—a man with not just one, but *two* PhDs in economics- and finance-related fields (#Jealous #LifeGoals). He understands markets better than anyone I've ever met. But even he wasn't immune to fear. He told us how he would come into his class of doctoral students during the '08 crash and say, half-joking but half-serious, that he needed to sell his investments before he lost everything. And every class period, his students would remind him of what he had taught *them*: remember the evidence, trust the process, and stay the course.

He admitted to my classmates and me that without those reminders, he might have caved to the panic. That story stuck with me, because it reminded me that knowledge alone isn't always enough. You need structure, support, and systems in place to help your rational mind win when emotions are screaming at you to jump ship. Don't underestimate fear's ability to steer you off course even when you know better.

So how do you actually stay the course when things get scary? When the market is crashing and your brain is screaming at you to sell before it gets worse? Here are a couple of tips you can try:

First, do what Marcus did—turn off the news.

Seriously. Stop watching the market crash. Stop refreshing your portfolio. Stop reading every gloomy headline predicting the end of the financial world. Ignorance really is bliss in this case. When prices are falling, obsessing over them just fuels the panic. In the age of social media, this can be harder than it sounds. Your feed will be full of hot takes and "urgent" updates. But the less you expose yourself to the noise, the easier it is to stick with your plan.

This only applies to your long-term investments; the money you've set aside for retirement, your future self, or goals that are still years away. If you're investing for something short-term, like next year's tuition or a down payment in six months, that money probably shouldn't be in the stock market at all. Short-term goals need safety and stability, not market swings. So when you see stocks dropping, remind yourself that the money you're watching go up and down isn't money you need right now. Stop watching and let it do its thing. You just need to keep going.

Second, do what my mentor did and phone a friend.

This might surprise you, but nearly all of the financial experts I know have someone they turn to for financial advice when things get emotional. One of my mentors put it perfectly: "My planner's best trait is that he's not me. He can be rational when I'm too emotional to think clearly." You don't necessarily need a credentialed professional. You just need a trusted friend or partner—someone you've talked to in advance, someone who understands your plan, and someone who's agreed to be your voice of reason when the fear kicks in.

Financial professionals don't lean on others because they lack knowledge. They do it because they know how powerful fear can be. They know the research and data. They know the stock market history. But they also know they can't out-muscle the powerful emotional systems of their brain that kick in under stress. When fear takes the wheel, rational thinking gets shoved into the backseat or kicked out of the car entirely. Even the smartest investors can make terrible decisions if they're relying on gut feelings in a crisis.

That's why having a trusted person to talk to—someone calm, clear-headed, and emotionally detached—can make all the difference. That person doesn't have to be immune to fear themselves. In fact, they'll probably be feeling fear too. But here's the magic: When they're talking to *you* about *your* money, they can think more clearly. They're not in the thick of your emotional storm, so they can calmly remind you of the facts. And when *they* feel rattled about *their* money, you can return the favor. You'll be the rational voice for them. When it matters most, that kind of partnership where you each keep the other grounded is one of the most powerful tools for staying the course.

Remember, DCA is a long-term strategy. It's about gradual accumulation, not instant results. The power of DCA lies in its simplicity and in the disciplined approach it brings to investing. Notice in the chart that the black DCA line goes below the gray line for a while. You're going to have to tough it out and watch your balance fall. But if you hang on, wait it out, and continue to invest even when the market is down, the rewards are immense. So keep your long-term perspective and don't get scared!

MOMENTS OF CLARITY

- **Dollar cost averaging (DCA) makes smart investing automatic.** With DCA, you invest a set amount on a regular schedule no matter what the market is doing. It takes emotion, timing, and guesswork out of the equation. You just set it and forget it.

- **DCA turns volatility into opportunity.** When the market drops, you buy more shares. When prices are high, you buy fewer. Over time, this naturally lowers your average cost and helps boost long-term returns.

- **You win by staying in the game.** DCA doesn't give you the *highest* returns possible, but it gives you *real* returns in the *real world*—with far less stress and far better consistency. Over time, consistency beats cleverness.

- **When in doubt, do nothing.** Market going up? Do nothing. Market crashing? Still do nothing. Just keep your automatic investments going and trust the process. DCA isn't just a good strategy, it's a great one—because it helps you *actually stick with it*!

CHAPTER EIGHTEEN

SELECTING THE RIGHT INVESTMENTS

By this point in my life, a lot of my memories of college are a bit hazy. But there is one lecture I remember clearly.

I was sitting in the second row of my Investments class, arms crossed, a little skeptical. We were discussing mutual funds, and my professor had just said something that made me frown.

"The manager's skill doesn't really matter much," he said. "What matters most is cost."

I raised my hand. "Wait—how can that be true? You're telling me the fund manager's ability to choose good stocks doesn't affect performance?"

He smiled, and I had the feeling that I'd just fallen into some sort of trap. "Ah," he said, "you've just stumbled onto one of the great debates of modern finance. If anyone ever truly found the secret to consistently picking winning stocks—reliably, ahead of time—it would be the holy grail. Instant riches. Nigh unlimited wealth."

He leaned against the desk. "The best minds in finance have been chasing that secret for decades. Actually, centuries. From ancient merchants in Babylon to Wall Street quants today, everyone's tried to find a consistent edge. And you know what they've found?"

I waited. I wasn't going to fall into another trap.

"That no one can consistently beat the market. Not after costs."

He paused, letting it sink in.

"Think about it. If a manager *could* beat the market reliably, they'd get rich, close their fund, and manage their own money. And if someone *did* discover a magic formula, the moment it became known, everyone would use it—and it would stop working."

He walked over to the whiteboard and scrawled one word: *cost*.

"That's the one factor you *can* control. And over time, the data is clear. The more you pay in fees, the worse your investment returns are likely to be. Not just sometimes—consistently. It's the only sure bet in investing."

I looked down at the prospectus I'd brought to class as part of a homework assignment. Expense ratio: 1.2 percent. Was that high? At the time, I had no idea.

"So if you want to be a smart investor," he said, "forget chasing star managers. Focus on the one edge that actually works: keeping your costs low."

That was my first exposure to a vital investing lesson. When it comes to choosing a mutual fund, many investors get lost in a sea of complexities like the fund manager's pedigree, past performance, and market predictions. However, research shows that these factors often amount to noise rather than useful information. The real game changers? Fees and expenses.

THE IMPACT OF FEES AND EXPENSES

Fees and expenses are not just small deductions—nickels and dimes you don't have to worry about. They're the anchors that will drag down your investment returns over time. Studies have consistently shown a negative relationship between high fees and fund performance.[15] In other words, the more you pay, the less you will earn.

So what is it about fees that can eat into your hard-earned money? Let's look at a list of the top reasons why fees actually matter more than performance:

- Predicting Future Performance Is a Guessing Game: Past performance is not a reliable indicator of future results. The market's ups and downs often render previous successes irrelevant.

- Fund Managers Rarely Beat the Market: Over the long term, actively managed funds seldom outperform the market index fund. Paying more for active management doesn't necessarily translate into better returns. So why pay extra? Research has found that at most, only 3 percent of professional mutual fund managers manage to beat the market index after you pay their fees.[16]

- Fees Eat Into Your Returns: Every dollar paid in fees is a dollar that isn't growing for your future. Over years or decades, this can amount to a significant loss in potential earnings.

15   Mark Grinblatt and Sheridan Titman, "The Persistence of Mutual Fund Performance," *The Journal of Finance* 47, no. 5 (1992): 1977–1984, https://doi.org/10.1111/j.1540-6261.1992.tb04692.x.

16   Eugene F. Fama and Kenneth R. French, "Luck Versus Skill in the Cross-Section of Mutual Fund Returns," *The Journal of Finance* 65, no. 5 (2010): 1915–1947, https://doi.org/10.1111/j.1540-6261.2010.01598.x.

THE EXPENSE RATIO

So how do you know if a fund is expensive or not? Every fund has what's called an *expense ratio*. This expense ratio is the cost of the fund. Think of it as the price tag. The higher the expense ratio, the more expensive the fund.

The expense ratio is a percentage of the balance you will be charged each year. So if your fund has a 2 percent expense ratio, the mutual fund company will charge you a fee equal to 2 percent of your balance each year. Unfortunately, finding a fund's expense ratio isn't always as easy as it should be. The most reliable place to look is in your brokerage's list of available mutual funds. Most brokerages let you filter or sort that list by expense ratio. Use that feature if it's available. It's one of the quickest ways to spot the low-cost options. For full step-by-step instructions on how to open a brokerage account and find those low-fee funds, check out Chapter 21 ("Action Plan for Investing").

If you're going to pay a fee for your investment, you should at least know what you are paying for. The fees in a mutual fund's expense ratio cover the ongoing costs of managing the fund, including the salary of the fund manager and investment research team, who select and monitor the fund's holdings. They also pay for administrative services like recordkeeping, customer service, and regulatory compliance. Some of the fees may go toward marketing the fund to other investors, and in some cases they can also cover things like travel expenses, conferences, and other costs that aren't directly tied to improving investor returns. While some of these activities may support the fund's operations, they don't usually translate into better performance for you, the investor.

While 1 or 2 percent sounds cheap, it stacks up over time. The chart below lays it out in stark detail. After thirty years, just a 1 percent annual fee can reduce your total balance by nearly 20 percent. And if you're paying a 2 percent fee, then you'd be down over 30 percent. That's money gone—silently skimmed from your future. And the worst part? You'll probably never know it happened. These fees don't show up as a line item or an alert; they quietly drain your returns year after year. Unless you see a breakdown like this, you'd never know how much those "tiny" percentages are costing you.

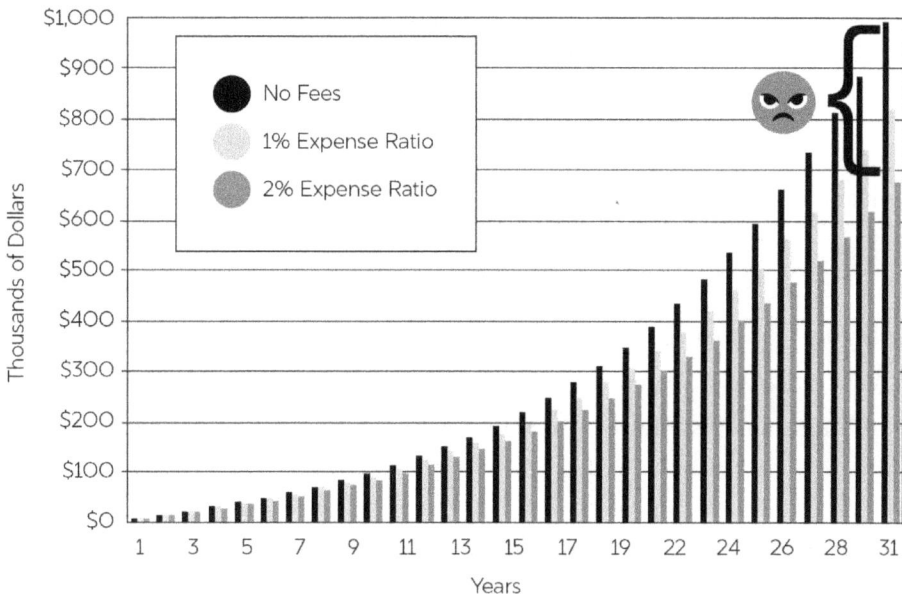

FIGURE 18.1. The cost of expense ratios.
Note how they eat into your returns over time.

WHERE TO FIND LOW-COST INVESTMENTS

So what's the solution? Simple: get the lowest fee possible. If there's one golden rule of investing that is actually supported by mountains of evidence, it's this: The lower the cost, the better your odds of success. Every dollar you don't pay in fees is a dollar that stays in your account, compounding over time.

The cheapest funds you can (and should) invest in are index mutual funds and ETFs. What are these funds?

INDEX FUNDS

An index fund is a type of mutual fund that doesn't try to pick the best stocks. Instead, it simply copies a market index. If the index goes up, the fund goes up. If the index goes down, so does the fund. The most famous example of a stock market index is the S&P 500—a list of 500 of the largest publicly traded companies in the US. An S&P 500 index fund just buys all 500 stocks in the same proportions as the index. No guessing, no forecasting, no expensive research. Just match the market index.

Because there's no active management, no team of researchers, no highly paid manager, the fees are incredibly low—often a tenth of a percent or less. Compare that to actively managed funds that charge 1 percent or more, and it's clear why index funds are a smart long-term bet.

EXCHANGE-TRADED FUNDS (ETFS)

These are like index funds in disguise. They usually track an index, just like an index fund, but they trade on the stock exchange like individual stocks. That means you can buy and sell them throughout the day at market prices, rather than waiting until the end of the trading day like you do with mutual funds. This makes them slightly different than index funds, but the differences are negligible for the average investor. It is safe for you to consider them functionally identical to index funds.

ETFs tend to have rock-bottom fees—sometimes even lower than index mutual funds. And they offer flexibility. Want to invest in US stocks? Global stocks? Bonds? Real estate? There's an ETF for just about everything. Investing doesn't have to be complicated. A simple, low-cost index fund or ETF can be a powerful tool in your investment arsenal. By choosing a fund that tracks a major market index at the lowest possible cost, you're positioning yourself to maximize returns without the hassle of trying to pick "winning" funds.

EMPHASIZE LOW FEES WITH TARGET DATE FUNDS

We've established the rule: Keep costs as low as possible. That's the golden guideline for picking mutual funds and ETFs. Lower fees mean higher returns, period. But remember what I said earlier? Every rule has an exception. Well, this rule is no exception to the "no exceptions" rule. The exception here is target date funds.

Target date funds will cost a little more than plain index funds or ETFs. But in this case, you're actually getting something valuable for that extra fee—automation, simplicity, and a built-in plan that adjusts as you get closer to retirement. That can be well worth the small price bump.

UNDERSTANDING TARGET DATE FUNDS

Target date funds (TDFs) are a type of mutual fund that automatically adjusts its asset allocation as you get closer to a specific retirement date (the target date). Early in your career, the fund might be more aggressive, investing more in stocks. But as you approach retirement, it gradually shifts to more conservative investments like bonds. These are truly ideal for saving for retirement. Just pick the fund whose target date corresponds to the approximate year you think you might retire, and *bam*! You're done.

For example, let's say you were born in the year 2000. You might want to pick a fund with a target date in 2070. This fund will automatically rebalance your investments every year on the assumption that you will retire in the year 2070, when you are 70 years old.

THE VALUE OF AUTOMATIC REBALANCING

Managers of target date funds take care of rebalancing as you get closer to retirement. Here are some advantages of that automatic approach:

- **Set It and Forget It:** TDFs provide a hands-off approach to investing. You choose a fund based on your expected retirement year, and the fund does the rest.

- **Strategic Asset Allocation:** The automatic shift from aggressive to conservative investments aligns with the typical investor's changing risk tolerance as they near retirement. This shift profoundly increases your chances of retiring successfully. (How it does this is quite complicated and beyond the scope of this book. Look up "sequence of returns" and "equity glidepath," or pick up a copy of *Everything You Need to Know About Retirement Income in One Little Book* from strategicmoneymethod.com if you are curious to know more.)

EXPENSE RATIOS IN TARGET DATE FUNDS

While we've discussed the value of sticking to funds with low fees, TDFs are a scenario where paying slightly more can be justifiable. The convenience and strategic (automatic) asset allocation offered by TDFs can offset the slightly higher expenses. But the goal with picking a TDF is still the same as with index funds or ETFs: Get the cheapest one you can. Log in to your investment account and shop around for less expensive options.

Even with TDFs, the expense ratio should be reasonable. A ratio of no more than 0.15 percent is a good benchmark. (Read that carefully—it's zero-point-one-five percent, not fifteen percent.) Some TDFs come with higher fees, but it's not really necessary to pay more. What's important is the date the fund targets. You're not shopping for the fanciest or best target date fund. All TDFs with the same target date will implement strategies that are similar enough as to make no substantial difference to you. So get the cheap one!

ROBOADVISING: REMOVING THE EMOTION

A relatively new strategy to help investors navigate the maze of investment options is to utilize a type of brokerage called a *roboadvisor*. Roboadvisors take the human element out of investing. They set an investment policy and then let the algorithm follow it for you.

There are two advantages to this: (1) Algorithms have no emotions, and emotional trading is the number one killer of investor success; and (2) it's considerably cheaper than hiring a human to do the work. These brokerages charge very low fees to give you the best effects of a target date fund, but with even less work on your part and even more benefits from more sophisticated investing techniques.

You literally just tell them when you want to retire and how much risk you feel you can handle, and the algorithm does the rest, following the latest science-based best practices available. It's a fantastic combination, and their track record is looking great so far.

The two best-known roboadvisors are Wealthfront and Betterment. But roboadvising is expanding, and some of the larger brokerages are starting to offer it in addition to their traditional accounts. Log in to your brokerage to see if they offer something like this.

MOMENTS OF CLARITY

- **Fees are the most reliable predictor of investment performance.** The lower the expense ratio, the better your odds of long-term success.

- **The expense ratio matters**—over thirty years, even a 1 percent fee can cost you 20 to 30 percent of your wealth. That's money lost quietly, invisibly, and unnecessarily.

- **Find the cheapest index fund or ETF your brokerage offers.** These types of funds are supposed to have inherently low costs— but double-check. Just because a fund is an ETF doesn't mean it *must* be inexpensive, only that it *should* be. Confirm the expense ratio of any fund you are thinking of using.

- **Target date funds are a justifiable exception.** You pay a bit more, but you get automation, rebalancing, and a plan that's aligned with your retirement timeline.

- **Roboadvising is a viable option.** Roboadvisors can give you many of the same benefits as target date funds but can often be less expensive and more tax efficient.

- **Investing doesn't need to be complicated.** The simplest, cheapest strategies are usually the best. Set your plan, automate it, and focus your attention on something more exciting than stock picking.

CHAPTER NINETEEN

RETIREMENT ACCOUNTS

L et's say you've started investing. Congrats! You've learned how to plant financial seeds, scatter them across different asset classes, and maybe even water them with regular contributions. That's investing in general: getting your money to grow.

But now it's time to step up your gardening game.

Because planting is good—but if you want a thriving, reliable harvest in the future, you need more than just soil and sunshine. You need a greenhouse.

Retirement accounts are like greenhouses; they're specialized environments designed to help your investments grow faster, stronger, and more predictably over the long term. They're protected from the harshest financial elements, like taxes—and temptation. They give your seeds the time and shelter they need to become something substantial.

You could technically plant your seeds anywhere, just like you could technically leave your retirement money in a regular investment account.

But why expose your fragile little seedlings to every storm, frost, and pest the financial world throws your way? Retirement accounts offer structure, insulation, and long-term care that regular investing doesn't.

Think of your retirement savings as a can of beans. The beans represent your hard-earned dollars, and the can is the investments you store them in. Now, what truly makes a difference is the label on the can—which (in our analogy) is the type of retirement account you choose. This label determines how your beans (dollars) are taxed; and as we'll see, the right label can mean paying fewer or even no taxes at all.

Because retirement accounts are not just storage vessels for your investments. They are powerful tools for tax savings. Whether you pay taxes now or later depends on the type of account you choose.

UNDERSTANDING THE TAX LABELS: TYPES OF RETIREMENT ACCOUNTS

- **Traditional IRA and 401(k):** These are like labels that say Pay Taxes Later. You contribute pre-tax income, which reduces your taxable income now and defers your tax payment until withdrawal in retirement.

- **Roth IRA and Roth 401(k):** These labels read Pay Taxes Now, Not Later. You contribute after-tax income, so you do pay taxes; you just do it before you deposit the money. This means your withdrawals, including earnings, are tax-free in retirement.

- **SEP IRAs and Solo 401(k)s for the Self-Employed:** Similar to a traditional IRA or 401(k) in terms of tax treatment, but with higher contribution limits, these are ideal for those with significant self-employment income.

There are dozens of other types of retirement accounts, but you are unlikely to ever meet them, and even less likely to need to know the specific details of how they work. Just know that if an employer offers a retirement plan, it's going to save you lots of money in taxes, no matter what type it is. So definitely use it!

THE MAGIC OF TAX DEFERRAL AND TAX-FREE GROWTH

Let's delve into why these tax labels matter so much:

- **Tax Deferral (Traditional Accounts):** By deferring taxes, you lower your current taxable income. Your investments grow tax-deferred, and you only pay taxes when you withdraw the money. This can be beneficial if you're in a lower tax bracket in retirement.

- **Tax-Free Growth (Roth Accounts):** With Roth accounts, you pay taxes up-front. However, the beauty lies in their tax-free growth. Imagine your beans growing without the taxman taking a share later on—that's what Roth offers.

Which is better? The answer is, it depends. Roths offer a little more flexibility; but from a tax perspective, the two types are very, very similar. The extra flexibility is the main reason why people tend to prefer Roth accounts over traditional accounts, but you really can't go wrong with either!

ILLUSTRATING THE VALUE OF TAX SAVINGS

Many people underestimate the amount of money that taxes will cost them in their retirement account. In the long run, the costs can be tremendous. The amount you will lose to taxes will of course depend on a number of factors; but as a very rough rule of thumb, you can expect a taxable account to lose between 20 and 30 percent of its value due to taxes. That's huge! When I say you should definitely use a retirement account (traditional IRA or Roth IRA) to save for retirement, that advice alone could save you hundreds of thousands of dollars in taxes.

The chart below shows the growth of two investment accounts that are identical except in one way: one is taxable and the other is a tax-advantaged retirement account. In this case, the investor lost nearly $600,000 in value from the account due to taxes. And the worst part? They probably don't even know it. They probably are just wondering why they don't have more money without realizing that taxes were eating away at their investments this whole time.

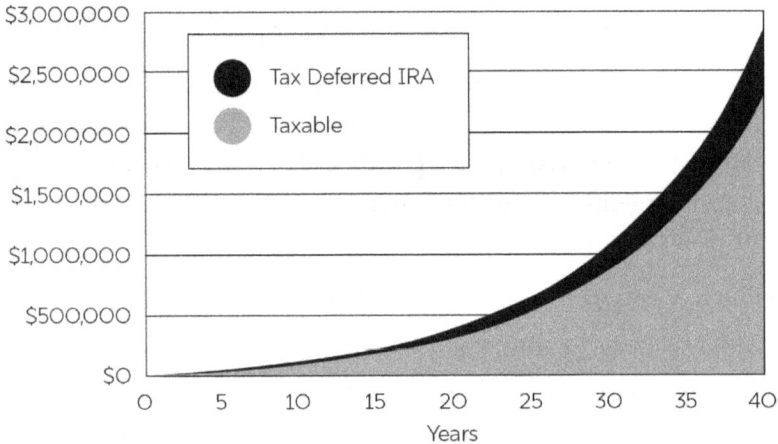

FIGURE 19.1. The Effect of Taxes on Your Investments. After 40 years, the tax-deferred account has over $560,000 more in it. That represents a 28% loss due to taxes. This is what makes retirement accounts such as Roth IRAs, traditional IRAs, 401(k)s, 403(b)s, etc., far better accounts for your wallet than nonretirement brokerage accounts!

EMPLOYER-SPONSORED PLANS VERSUS INDIVIDUAL PLANS

Most retirement accounts can't be created by individuals. These are called *employer-sponsored* plans, and that means that only your employer can create one. Employer-sponsored plans include 401(k)s, 403(b)s, Keoghs, SEP IRAs, SIMPLE IRAs, and pensions. If your employer offers you one of these plans, definitely use it! These plans not only have the possibility of letting you get more money from your employer through a match (or them just putting free money in it for you!), but they also have high contribution limits.

On the other hand, individual (non-employer) IRAs can be opened by anyone who has income from a job, or who is married to someone who has a job. This gives you lots of control and freedom to choose both the type of IRA and the investment options. But their big downside is that they have low contribution limits.

All retirement accounts have a limit to how much you can put in each year. These are called *contribution limits*, and they change each year. For example, as I write this in 2025, IRAs have a limit of $7,000, while employer-sponsored plans like 401(k)s have limits around $23,500. (If you find yourself saving tons of money, you can google the current limits.)

CHOOSING THE RIGHT LABEL FOR YOUR ACCOUNTS

Selecting the optimal retirement account for your situation can be a complicated process that involves examining tax rates, trying to predict political trends, and otherwise forecasting the future. But it doesn't have to be. What really matters is that you use a retirement account, period. Which kind you choose generally only makes a little bit of difference. If your employer offers a 401(k) . . . *use it!* If they offer a pension, *use it!* If they offer a SIMPLE IRA, *use it!* If you're not sure what they offer, contact HR. They should be able to help you get started in the company-sponsored plan if they have one. If they don't offer any of these, then start your own IRA or Roth IRA . . . and *USE IT!*

HOW TO START AN IRA

Starting an IRA is actually easier than you might imagine. We'll cover the full process in Chapter 21, but this brief outline shows how simple it can be to get started:

1. **Select a Brokerage:** A brokerage is a company that buys and sells investments for you and manages your investment accounts. Think of them like normal banks that offer investment accounts instead of checking accounts. You want to select a brokerage that charges the lowest fees possible. Good choices are Vanguard, Fidelity, Wealthfront, and Betterment. Each of these companies offers different tools and resources, but they also charge different fees. They are each very affordable and reputable, which is why I list them here.

2. **Select an Account Type:** Like a bank, the brokerage's website should have a great big button that says something like *Open an account*. It'll be easy to find, because they *want* you to find it. Click that button and then follow the steps. At some point they will ask you what type of account you want, or what the account is for. Select the IRA that you want, or select "retirement" if they ask for the purpose of the account. And that's it! Account created.

3. **Select an Investment:** Now that you have an account, you need to send some money and tell the brokerage which investments you want. They each have their own process for doing this, but you want to use the tools they have to find investments that meet the criteria we discussed earlier. (In case you forgot: You want a low-cost ETF, index fund, or target date fund.)

Voilà! Now you have an IRA with some investments in it. Set up your automatic deposits from your regular bank to your brokerage, and you're done. Just sit back, relax, and wait for those investments to grow.

LIFE INSURANCE AS AN INVESTMENT

You might come across a financial advisor—or more accurately, an insurance salesperson—pitching a life insurance policy as a retirement investment. The pitch usually starts with phrases like *It's like a Roth IRA, but without the income limits!* or *Tax-free growth with no market downside!* And to be fair, life insurance policies do offer some appealing tax benefits.

Like a Roth 401(k) or a Roth IRA, permanent life insurance (such as indexed universal or whole-life policies) allows for tax-deferred growth of the money inside the policy. If structured correctly, it can also provide tax-free withdrawals via loans against the policy's cash value. That combination—tax-deferred growth and tax-free access—sounds a lot like the perks of Roth accounts or employer retirement plans. On top of that, your family would get a guaranteed life insurance payment when you die, no matter how old you are when that happens.

Sound too good to be true? It is.

BEWARE OF THE FEES!

The most substantial drawback to using life insurance as an investment is the cost of the fees. Life insurance–based investment plans come with extremely high and often difficult-to-see costs. There are fees for administration, commissions, mortality charges, riders, surrender charges, and more. The cost structure is rarely spelled out clearly in the glossy brochure or sales pitch—because if it were, most people would walk away.

Unlike a 401(k), where you can see your fund expense ratios, or a Roth IRA, where you can choose low-cost index funds, the internal costs of insurance policies are buried in legalese and require a magnifying glass (and an actuary) to decipher. Research has shown that for households in the middle to upper-middle income brackets, the tax cost on a well-managed taxable investment account is often lower than the internal fees charged by most cash-value life insurance policies.[17] If you're investing in low-cost index funds and holding them long-term, your tax hit can be minimal, especially with the preferential rates on long-term capital gains and qualified dividends.

It's a bit ironic, really. Life insurance policies are often sold on the promise of tax advantages—but the truth is, most households already have plenty of tax-advantaged investment options available, and without steep insurance fees. In 2025, a married couple where just one spouse has access to a 401(k) from their employer can still shelter up to $37,500 in retirement accounts: $23,500 in the 401(k), plus $7,000 in an IRA for each spouse. Unless you're already maxing that out, there's simply no need to chase additional tax shelters.

BETTER WAYS TO INVEST

So why do so many people fall for the life insurance pitch? Because these policies are sold, not sought. Insurance salespeople are trained to make these policies sound like the smartest financial move you could ever make. They have polished scripts, emotionally compelling stories, and just enough truth to sound convincing. And to be fair, these policies aren't inherently bad. But for most households, there are simpler, cheaper, and much more efficient ways to invest.

And if you are saving more than $37,500 a year? Congratulations, you're doing exceptionally well. But at that point, your situation is probably complex enough that it's worth bringing in a fee-only financial

---

17   Jordan H. Smith, "Analyzing the Value of Life Insurance as an Investment," *Journal of Financial Planning* 27, no. 3 (2014): 22–23, https://www.financialplanningassociation.org/article/journal/MAR14-analyzing-value-life-insurance-investment-0.

planner to help you navigate your options. You don't need a policy—you need a professional.

To be fair, there are some clever advanced financial strategies that use life insurance in powerful ways. High-net-worth individuals sometimes use permanent life insurance to reduce estate taxes, provide liquidity for their heirs, structure charitable giving, or even create tax-efficient retirement income. When these strategies are used well, they can be incredibly effective.

These strategies are powerful, but they're also very complex, so to work as intended, they generally need to be handled by true professionals—people who specialize in estate law, tax planning, and fiduciary financial advice. These aren't one-size-fits-all solutions. They're finely tuned tools for people with very specific planning needs and the resources to hire the right experts.

THE BENEFITS OF TERM LIFE INSURANCE

As for the rest of us? We don't need a complicated wealth transfer strategy. We just need to make sure our families are protected if something happens to us. We need a way to build long-term wealth that's simple, flexible, and cost-effective. That's exactly what term life insurance and low-cost investing offer.

Term life insurance is simple. You pay a small monthly premium, and in return your loved ones receive a large death benefit if you die during the coverage period. That's it. No cash value. No hidden fees. Just pure protection.

And here's where the magic happens: Instead of pouring thousands of dollars into a permanent policy weighed down by fees, you invest that extra money into a Roth IRA, your 401(k), or a taxable brokerage account. Over time, that invested money compounds, and you end up with far more wealth and flexibility than you would have inside a cash-value policy.

MOMENTS OF CLARITY

- **Retirement accounts are the greenhouses of investing.** They don't grow different investments—they just give your investments better conditions in which to thrive, mostly thanks to tax advantages.

- **Tax savings can be worth hundreds of thousands of dollars.** Over a few decades, a tax-advantaged retirement account can outperform a taxable one by a six-figure margin. That's money that stays in your pocket instead of going to the IRS.

- **If your employer offers a plan—*use it*.** Whether it's a 401(k), 403(b), SIMPLE IRA, or pension, don't overthink it. These plans offer higher contribution limits, possible employer contributions, and excellent tax advantages.

- **Don't wait for perfect. Just start.** The biggest mistake isn't picking the "wrong" type of retirement account; it's not using one at all. Start somewhere—your future self will thank you.

- **Buy term life insurance and invest the difference.** Permanent life insurance policies (like whole life, variable life, or universal life) can offer some advanced financial strategies, but their high fees make them too costly to serve as ideal investment vehicles for most people.

CHAPTER TWENTY

COMMON INVESTMENT PITFALLS

As you embark on your investment journey, you can avoid costly mistakes by being aware of common pitfalls and knowing how to avoid them. This chapter is dedicated to helping you steer clear of the traps that ensnare many investors (although simply following the strategies we have already discussed will automatically help you avoid these pitfalls).

PITFALL 1: TRYING TO TIME THE MARKET

Many investors believe they can predict the market's highs and lows. This practice of guessing when the market is about to crash and when it's about to skyrocket is called *timing the market*. However, timing the market is beyond difficult, even for professionals. In fact, the research suggests that it is just shy of completely impossible, although many stock market gurus naturally disagree with this assessment.[18]

The problem is, trying to guess when the market will crash can have extremely bad results. Research shows that 90 percent of the returns produced by the stock market are produced on 10 percent of the days.[19]

---

18 Thousands of studies have been conducted and found no (or at best, very little) evidence of fund manager skill benefiting investors. See, for example: Jack L. Treynor and Kay Mazuy, "Can Mutual Funds Outguess the Market?," *Harvard Business Review* 44, no. 4 (1966): 131–136; Roy D. Henriksson and Robert C. Merton, "On Market Timing and Investment Performance. II. Statistical Procedures for Evaluating Forecasting Skills," *Journal of Business* 54, no. 4 (1981): 513–533, https://doi.org/10.1086/296144; Roy D. Henriksson, "Market Timing and Mutual Fund Performance: An Empirical Investigation," *Journal of Business* 57, no. 1 (1984): 73–96, http://doi.org/10.1086/296225; Bruce N. Lehmann and David M. Modest, "Mutual Fund Performance Evaluation: A Comparison of Benchmarks and Benchmark Comparisons," *Journal of Finance* 42, no. 2 (1987): 233–265, https://doi.org/10.1111/j.1540-6261.1987.tb02566.x; Kent Daniel, Mark Grinblatt, Sheridan Titman, and Russ Wermers, "Measuring Mutual Fund Performance with Characteristic-Based Benchmarks," *Journal of Finance* 52, no. 3 (1997): 1035–1058, https://doi.org/10.1111/j.1540-6261.1997.tb02724.x; Lawrence Kryzanowski, Simon Lalancette, and Minh Chau To, "Performance Attribution Using an APT with Prespecified Macrofactors and Time-Varying Risk Premia and Betas," *Journal of Financial and Quantitative Analysis* 32, no. 2 (1997): 205–224, https://doi.org/10.2307/2331173; William N. Goetzmann, Massimo Massa, and K. Geert Rouwenhorst, "Behavioral Factors in Mutual Fund Flows," Working Paper No. ysm135, Yale School of Management, 2000; Wolfgang Bessler, David Blake, Peter Lückoff, and Ian Tonks, "Why Is Persistent Mutual Fund Performance So Difficult to Achieve? The Impact of Fund Flows and Manager Turnover," Working Paper presented at the European Financial Management Association 2009 Annual Meeting, Milan, February 10, 2009; Campbell R. Harvey and Yan Liu, "Luck Versus Skill in the Cross-Section of Mutual Fund Returns: Reexamining the Evidence," *Journal of Finance* 77, no. 3 (2022): 1921–1966, https://doi.org/10.1111/jofi.13123.

19 Hubert Dichtl, Wolfgang Drobetz, and Lawrence Kryzanowski, "Timing the Stock Market: Does It Really Make No Sense?," *Journal of Behavioral and Experimental Finance* 10 (2016): 88–104, https://doi.org/10.1016/j.jbef.2016.03.005.

If you miss that critical 10 percent of days because you were 100 percent certain the market was going to crash and sold your stocks, you are going to put a major dent in your returns!

- **Solution:** Stick to a long-term investment strategy and resist the urge to buy or sell based on short-term market movements. Research is clear: Time *in* the market (i.e., buying stocks and holding them for a long time) is generally far more effective than *timing* the market. The dollar cost averaging technique automatically lets you buy more when prices are low and less when prices are high. Don't guess, and don't panic, and definitely don't sell. Just keep investing every month regardless of what's going on in the economy.

$1,000 Invested in the MSCI Global Index on January 1, 2001

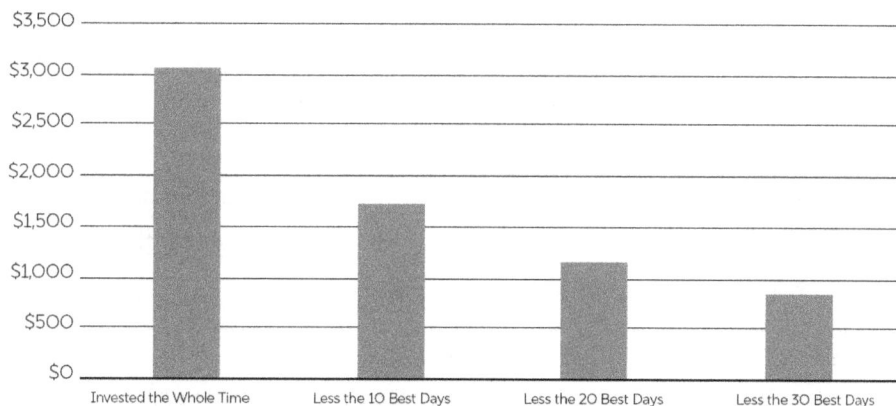

FIGURE 20.1. Effect of missing just a few days in the market.
(Source: Schroders)[20]

---

20 David Brett, "The Cost of Trying to Time the Markets Since 2001," Schroders, February 13, 2020, https://www.schroders.com/en-us/us/individual/insights/the-real-risk-of-trying-to-time-the-market/.

PITFALL 2: CHASING PAST PERFORMANCE

Investors often select investments based solely on past returns. A winner yesterday should be a winner today, after all. That's what our common sense tells us. However, it doesn't work like that with investments. Past performance is not indicative of future results. A fund that did well last year might not do well this year. In fact, research has shown that the better an investment has done recently, the more likely it is to do poorly in the near future.[21]

- **Solution:** Focus on your own investment goals and risk tolerance, and the fund's overall fit with your portfolio. Just buy broad market ETF or target date fund and don't be tempted by the lure of fantastic returns. Remember, if it sounds too good to be true, it probably is.

PITFALL 3: OVERLOOKING FEES AND EXPENSES

High fees can eat into your investment returns over time. Investors often overlook or underestimate the impact of fees. Even worse, some investors assume that because a fund is expensive, it must be better. An expensive manager must be a good manager . . . right? Exactly the opposite is true. Expensive funds are worse—period.

- **Solution:** Pay close attention to the expense ratios of any mutual funds, ETFs, or target date funds you are considering adding to your portfolio. Opt for low cost as much as possible, as we discussed in earlier chapters.

---

21   Grinblatt and Titman, "The Persistence of Mutual Fund Performance."

PITFALL 4: FAILING TO DIVERSIFY

Putting all your eggs in one basket is risky. If that investment performs poorly, your entire portfolio suffers.

- **Solution:** Diversify your investments across different asset classes and within asset classes (i.e., different sectors or regions). This can help reduce risk and smooth out returns. Buying a target date fund, or an index fund, or a broad market ETF automatically gives you a very effective level of diversification with no effort on your part!

PITFALL 5: LETTING EMOTIONS DRIVE DECISIONS

Investing can be emotional, especially during market downturns. Fear and greed can lead to poor decision-making.

- **Solution:** Develop a sound investment plan and stick to it. Avoid making impulsive decisions based on market highs or lows. Phone a friend or stop watching the markets if you are feeling fearful, impulsive, greedy, or emotional in any way. Just stick to your dollar cost averaging strategy and keep on investing every month!

PITFALL 6: UNDERESTIMATING THE IMPACT OF TAXES

Expense ratios are a well-documented drag on the performance of your investments, and taxes are expense ratios on steroids. It's even more important to avoid taxes than it is to avoid high expense ratios, because tax rates tend to be much higher than expense ratios.

- **Solution:** Utilize retirement accounts for their tax benefits. If your employer offers access to a 401(k), 403(b), pension, or other retirement account, you should definitely use it. Contact your HR representative at work for details on what's available. You should also open a Roth IRA and use that!

PITFALL 7: INVESTING ON MARGIN

While creating your brokerage account, you may see options talking about creating a "margin." Margin trading is a complicated tool that basically lets you borrow investment money from your brokerage. In other words, it allows you to invest money you don't have. The effect is that it can multiply your investment results. When times are good, this is wonderful. However, times are not always good. And when things go bad, margin investing will also multiply your losses.

- **Solution:** If your brokerage at any point asks you to invest "on margin" or "in a margin account," follow the old advice and just say no! You do not need to use margin investing to get great investment results; and without a full understanding of how it works, you are much more likely to cause yourself more harm than good.

PITFALL 8: INVESTING IN THE LATEST TREND

Every investor is looking for one simple thing: a way to get rich quick without taking any risk. Unfortunately, this simple desire goes unfulfilled, because such an investment does not (and fundamentally *cannot*) exist. But that doesn't stop us from hoping and dreaming. This is why there is almost always some hot new investment, some great trend, some novel new idea in investing, floating around and promising to make us all rich.

The trouble is, if these things worked, there would be lots more rich people in the world. These get-rich-quick schemes and trendy investing ideas are always around. You don't even have to have your nose buried in *Forbes* magazine every month to hear about them. Some become so prevalent that they leak into society in general.

It's happened hundreds of times throughout history. It happened in the 1990s with Beanie Babies and these fancy new things called "internet stocks." It happened again with real estate from 2005 to 2007. These were all very popular investments because they promised to make their investors rich at no risk.

The latest big trend like this is cryptocurrency. You may have heard of the most famous cryptocurrency—Bitcoin. Bitcoin is famous for having made people rich, giving them millions of dollars in profits in a matter of a few weeks or months. With potential benefits like that, who wouldn't want to invest in Bitcoin and also get rich? I certainly would.

The problem with cryptocurrencies and other trendy investments is that you never hear the full story. For every Bitcoin millionaire there are thousands and thousands of others who have lost fortunes in Bitcoin. You don't hear about them very often because (1) people who lose money don't tend to shout their stories from the rooftops and (2) their stories are not usually very dramatic. They just bought at the wrong time and sold at the wrong time. The public loves a rags-to-riches story, and so our media only tells us those kinds of stories.

Maybe that's just Bitcoin, though? There are plenty of other cryptocurrencies you could buy, after all. Surely we can buy into those and ride them to riches and glory? Maybe, maybe not. You see, while stories about Bitcoin make us think that cryptocurrencies as a whole are the next big money maker, there is little to no evidence to support that claim.

Think about it. Can you name even one cryptocurrency other than Bitcoin? Most people can't. They hear the word "cryptocurrency" and think about Bitcoin, and then mistakenly assume that cryptocurrencies overall are similar to Bitcoin. The reality is that there were over 23,000 different cryptocurrencies available to choose from in 2023, and only four are worth more than $1 per coin. And only two have produced significant value for investors: Bitcoin and Ethereum. Not only that, but from 2013 to 2021, approximately 2,400 cryptocurrencies failed, and another 4,400 failed from 2021 to 2023.[22]

That means that in a ten-year span (2013 to 2023), there have been two huge successes and 6,800 complete failures out of about 29,800 total cryptocurrencies. That represents an astounding 0.00006 percent chance of picking a cryptocurrency that will make you rich, and about a 22 percent chance of your chosen cryptocurrency failing (and you losing 100 percent of the money you invested). In other words, you are 34,000 times more likely to lose everything on a cryptocurrency than you are to become rich.

While those are better odds than the lottery, they are *far* worse odds than the stock market. Not to mention that stocks can let you diversify (in a way that cryptocurrencies and other trendy investments usually cannot), thus giving you substantial protection against losses while giving consistent chances of long-term gain.

Long story short: Far more fortunes have been lost chasing these types of get-rich-quick investments than have been made. The headlines don't tell the whole story. Don't get caught up in the glitz and glam of instant fortunes. Take the boring but proven path of long-term growth.

- **Solution:** Just pick the types of investments I've talked about in this book (index fund, ETF, target date fund, or roboadvisor) and don't let your head get turned by the allure of quick money. As Shakespeare said, not all that glitters is gold. If you want to take some money in a separate little account and play some games gambling it on trendy investments, that's fine. But don't entrust your long-term financial safety to these fair-weather friends!

---

22   Brenden Rearick, "Crypto Graveyard: Thousands of Coins Listed in Recent Years Have Already Failed," Nasdaq, March 31, 2023, https://www.nasdaq.com/articles/crypto-graveyard:-thousands-of-coins-listed-in-recent-years-have-already-failed; David Chang, "Here's How Many Crypto Coins Failed Last Year," Motley Fool Money, May 31, 2023, https://www.fool.com/money/cryptocurrency/articles/heres-how-many-crypto-coins-failed-last-year/.

PITFALL 9: ROMANTICIZING REAL ESTATE

You've probably seen influencers on social media claiming that real estate is the only path to wealth. That's not just misleading—it's flat-out wrong. Real estate is often hyped online, but in reality it's riskier, more hands-on, and more complex than investing in mutual funds or ETFs.

Yes, real estate can offer tax advantages. But so can stocks and bonds, especially when held in tax-advantaged accounts like IRAs or 401(k)s. In fact, when used properly, retirement accounts can make stock investing even more tax-efficient than real estate.

To be clear: Real estate can be a valid investment choice. It has unique features that appeal to some people, such as leverage and the potential for steady cash flow. But to do it well, you'll need to put in serious work to learn about taxes, laws, local markets, maintenance, tenant management, and more. It's not passive income, unless you're outsourcing a lot of the work—and even then it comes with trade-offs.

So why do we put real estate on a pedestal? Partly because it's tangible. You can see it, touch it, walk through it. And monthly rent checks feel more "real" than dividends or capital gains. But don't be fooled. Stocks and bonds can also generate regular income, without the hassle of leaky roofs or late-night tenant calls. You don't have to invest in real estate to build wealth.

- **Solution:** At the end of the day, real estate isn't better or worse than other investments. It's just different. It comes with its own set of risks, costs, and headaches that rarely make it into the highlight reels on social media. Make your decision with eyes wide open, not just because someone online said it's the only way.

MOMENTS OF CLARITY

- **If it sounds too good to be true, it probably is.** Wild promises of high returns with no risk are a major red flag. Real investing involves patience, not magic.

- **Be skeptical of anyone selling a strategy or a secret.** If someone's trying to sell you an investment gimmick, their goal is to make money *off* you—not *for* you.

- **The best investments are boring—and that's a good thing.** You don't need hype or flashy pitches. What you *do* need is consistent, long-term growth. When it comes to building wealth, boring is beautiful.

CHAPTER TWENTY-ONE

ACTION PLAN FOR INVESTING

L et's distill everything we've learned about investing into simple, actionable steps to kickstart your journey towards financial growth and security.

STEP 1: OPEN A RETIREMENT ACCOUNT

Your first action is to open a retirement account. Choose the one that best suits your tax situation and financial goals, whether it's a 401(k) through your employer, a traditional IRA, or a Roth IRA. Remember, this account is not just a savings tool; it's your tax-advantaged gateway to long-term wealth accumulation.

STEP 2: SELECT AN AMOUNT TO INVEST EACH MONTH

Decide on a consistent amount you can comfortably invest each month. This shouldn't be an amount that stretches your budget too thin. It's important to maintain a balance between your current financial needs and your future goals.

STEP 3: INVEST IN A BROAD MARKET ETF, A TARGET DATE MUTUAL FUND, OR A ROBOADVISOR WITH A VERY LOW EXPENSE RATIO

Choose investment vehicles that are cost-effective and that align with your investment strategy. Broad market ETFs are great for diversified exposure to the stock market, while target date funds offer a more hands-off approach, automatically adjusting your asset allocation as you near retirement. Remember that a roboadvisor is a type of brokerage, so if you want to use a roboadvisor you will need to find a brokerage that markets itself as such. Wealthfront and Betterment are the largest roboadvisors, but there are a number of good options just a Google search away. To maximize your returns, always look for options with very low expense ratios, regardless of which type of investment you choose.

STEP 4: USE DOLLAR COST AVERAGING BY INVESTING THE SAME AMOUNT OF MONEY EACH MONTH AUTOMATICALLY

Implement dollar cost averaging (DCA) by investing your predetermined amount regularly, regardless of market fluctuations. This strategy can help smooth out the volatility of the market and mitigate the risk of investing a large amount at an inopportune time. Set up automatic contributions to make this process consistent and effortless.

FINDING INVESTMENT EXPENSE RATIOS

It's easy to say, "Find a broad market ETF or target date fund with a low expense ratio," but it can be a little daunting to try to actually implement this process. To give you an idea of what you should see when searching for an investment product, the QR code links below contain screenshots from three different brokerages. Each brokerage is a bit different, though, so think of these as examples of what to look for.

BROKERAGE 1: VANGUARD

Vanguard is a brokerage that is famous for its low-cost attitude towards investing. Scan the QR code to view steps on how to find mutual funds and their expense ratios on Vanguard's website.

Vanguard QR Code

BROKERAGE 2: FIDELITY

Fidelity is a very popular brokerage for company retirement plans like 401(k)s. If your employer offers a retirement plan, there is a decent chance that it's being hosted by Fidelity. Scan the QR code to view steps on how to find mutual funds and their expense ratios on Fidelity's website.

Fidelity QR Code

BROKERAGE 3: WEALTHFRONT—THE ROBOADVISOR

Wealthfront is a roboadvisor, so the process is going to be a lot more hands-off and user-friendly than with a traditional brokerage. Scan the QR code to view steps on how to find mutual funds and their expense ratios on Wealthfront's website!

Wealthfront QR Code

MOMENTS OF CLARITY

- **Investing is a marathon, not a sprint.** Focus on steady progress, not quick wins. Long-term success comes from patience and consistency.

- **Make informed, intentional choices.** The best investors aren't the luckiest—they're the most disciplined and most educated.

- **Stay focused on your long-term goals.** Keep your eyes on the big picture, even when markets get noisy.

- **You have the tools—now use them.** With what you've learned, you're now equipped to make smart decisions and build lasting financial security.

CONCLUSION

O ver the course of this book, we've built something deeper than a financial plan. We've built a way of thinking. You started by crafting a vision for the kind of life you want to lead, then used that vision to identify your values and set meaningful financial priorities.

We learned how to evaluate every money decision, big or small, by asking three simple but powerful questions:

- *What is the purpose of the purchase?*
- *Is it worth the cost?*
- *Is there a smart swap?*

We set up a spending strategy that puts your values at the center of your everyday choices, helping you navigate the noise and avoid decision fatigue.

We explored how debt isn't good or bad, but simply a tool—one that can either help you buy valuable time or quietly siphon away your future, depending on how it's used. We examined the hidden costs behind our purchases and the ways financing can obscure the true price we pay. We learned how to invest with confidence by focusing on low fees and broad diversification, and how to avoid the traps of speculation, sales pitches, and financial fads. And most importantly, we learned that personal finance isn't about following rigid rules—it's about thinking clearly, weighing trade-offs, and making decisions that align with what truly matters to you.

When things get truly complicated—and they will— it can also be wise to get help. There's no shame in bringing in a professional when you're in over your head. But be cautious. Not everyone offering financial advice is working in your best interest. Always follow the money. Ask how they get paid. Commission-based salespeople often face a painful conflict between what's best for you and what pays them the most. That's why I recommend looking for a Certified Financial Planner (CFP) when you need expert advice. CFPs are trained, tested, and held to a fiduciary standard, meaning they're legally obligated to put your interests first. Yes, you'll pay for their time—usually by the hour—but that fee buys unbiased advice, not a sales pitch. In many cases, a few hundred dollars' worth of good advice can lead to financial decisions that pay off by tens or even hundreds of thousands of dollars over your lifetime.

If there's one thing I hope you take away from this book, it's that financial success doesn't come from perfection or genius or extensive knowledge—it comes from intention and consistency. You don't need to be a spreadsheet wizard or be able to predict the stock market. You simply need to keep showing up.

Keep making thoughtful, value-driven decisions. Keep adjusting when life changes. Small steps, taken consistently, lead to big results. That's true whether you're trying to pay off debt, build savings, protect your family, or plan for retirement. Every choice matters. Every dollar has a job. And every day is another chance to take control.

These principles aren't meant to lock you into a rigid plan. They're meant to grow with you. Your life will change. Your income may rise or fall. Your goals will evolve. But if you keep coming back to this strategic method—if you keep asking the right questions, prioritizing what matters most, and making trade-offs with clarity—you'll stay on a path that leads to lasting security and fulfillment.

There's a moment in one of my favorite books where a character asks, *What's the most important step a person can take?* For a long while, he believes the answer that I also once believed—the first step, obviously! It's a profound moment in the book when that character realizes that the first step *isn't* the most important one. It's the *next* step. No matter how many missteps are behind you, no matter how overwhelmed or discouraged you've felt, you always have the power to choose a new path. One step. One decision. One choice in the right direction. And then another. And another.

So be patient with yourself. Changing your financial trajectory takes time. Adjusting habits and shifting your mindset is a process, not an overnight transformation. There will be missteps. You'll make mistakes. We all do. But failure is not the opposite of success—it's part of it. What matters is that you keep going. I've watched too many people climb out of financial chaos to ever believe that anyone is beyond hope. You are capable of more than you think.

Please believe in your ability to succeed. Financial security isn't reserved for the lucky, the wealthy, or the perfect. It's available to anyone willing to slow down, think clearly, and act with purpose. You now have the tools. You've done the hard work of understanding what really matters. And now, the rest is practice—day by day, decision by decision. This is your financial life. You get to shape it. This is your moment.

Take the next step towards a brighter future.

ACKNOWLEDGMENTS

This book wouldn't exist without the support of an incredible community of friends, mentors, teachers, and family. I owe so much of who I am to their guidance and encouragement.

To my parents—thank you for instilling in me the values of hard work and compassion. To my brothers, friends, and extended family—your encouragement has meant the world. I'm grateful for my brilliant mentors and colleagues at Texas Tech University, Western Carolina University, and the University of Arizona whose wisdom, passion, and keen perspectives helped shape me and, by extension, this work.

And above all, to my extraordinary wife, Jennie—your support carried me through even the most trying moments. Your steady support through every challenge, your unwavering faith in me, and your love gave me the strength to keep going. This journey was never mine alone—it was ours—and I am endlessly grateful for your love, your brilliance, and your strength through it all.

INDEX

ABOUT THE AUTHOR

PATRICK PAYNE, PHD, CFP®, is a financial educator, author, and advocate for clear and ethical guidance in personal finance. He holds a PhD in personal financial planning from Texas Tech University, an MBA from Utah Valley University, and dual bachelor's degrees in finance and economics from Utah State University. He currently teaches at the University of Arizona as an associate professor of practice in personal and family financial planning.

Patrick's passion for financial literacy grew out of frustration with the misleading advice and sales-driven tactics so common in the financial world. His work is dedicated to helping individuals and families make smarter decisions, avoid costly mistakes, and gain confidence with their money.

What fascinates him most is the powerful connection between money and human behavior. To him, personal finance isn't just about spreadsheets and savings accounts—it's about how people think, feel, and make choices. By blending practical financial strategies with insights into why we do what we do, Patrick equips readers with tools to build better habits, reduce stress, and align their money with what matters most.

For more tools and resources, visit his website at
strategicmoneymethod.com.

www.ingramcontent.com/pod-product-compliance
Lightning Source LLC
Chambersburg PA
CBHW031841200326
41597CB00012B/225